LITERARY WALKING TOURS OF

Gothic Dublin

LITERARY WALKING TOURS OF

Gothic Dublin

BY BRIAN J. SHOWERS

ILLUSTRATED BY DUANE SPURLOCK

FOREWORD BY PAT LIDDY

NONSUCH

First published 2006

Nonsuch Publishing Ltd
73 Lower Leeson Street
Dublin 2
Ireland
www.nonsuch-publishing.com

British Library Cataloguing in Publication Data.
A catalogue record for this book is available from the British Library.

ISBN 1 84588 523 6
13-ISBN 978 1 84588 523 6

Typesetting and origination by Tempus Publishing Limited
Printed in Great Britain

CONTENTS

For my grandmother,
who was patient enough to read the first book I
wrote when I was eight.

and

In memory of Jim Stuckey,
who taught me how to teach myself.

FOREWORD

Hidden beneath layers of outward respectability every metropolis has its quota of the weird, the eccentric, and the ghastly but perhaps Dublin has amassed more than its fair share. In the nineteenth century and earlier, its cobbled streets were poorly lit, its alleyways full of forbidding gloom. Grim tenements glowered over the warren of narrow streets and shadowy figures were silhouetted behind the drawn curtains of Georgian mansions. The poverty of the masses was accentuated by the constant political strife of the period. Through unceasing winter fogs, created by countless domestic and occasional industrial chimneys, barely relieved by the pavement gas lamps, beggars pitifully shuffled along their weary paths, assassins stalked their unsuspecting prey, government spies lurked in dim doorways and thieves prowled the back lanes seeking out their heartless opportunities.

Disease preyed upon almost every household, striking victims with tuberculosis, diphtheria and a host of childhood killers. The Great Famine of the 1840s and its dreadful aftermath, cholera, visited many a household. Under the spell of flickering candlelight, tales told about victims of cholera being buried alive fuelled many an active imagination. The gruesome reputation of certain places caused many a sensitive soul to shudder as they hurried past. Innocent-looking streets, squares, parks or buildings concealed murky or sadistic histories of gibbets and scaffolds, of beheading and torture, of restless spirits and demonic goings-on.

The city is not short of places to point out today where the past is spoken of in hushed whispers or with dire warnings; of encountering fiends by circulating the Black Church, of ghosts desperately searching for the unfound in Malahide Castle, in the Lord Mayor's Mansion House and in Marsh's Library; of black masses and devil worshipping in the Hell-Fire Club and of the bodies of criminals or leper and plague victims thrown on Misery Hill or in Blackpitts. Crypts, cloisters, towers, dungeons and graveyards all have their terrible secrets.

The Irish never needed facts to create a good story but insert into this enviable talent the presence of all of the above and it was inevitable that the potent cocktail of truth, concoction and folklore would produce a string of writers who would excel in the genre of the macabre and the gothic. Sure enough, out of the pantheon of renowned Dublin writers, a trio did emerge who excelled and even paved the future of this genre for the rest of the world. They were Charles Maturin, Joseph Sheridan Le Fanu and the great Bram Stoker, creator of *Dracula*.

Brian J. Showers has done this city and the literature of the gothic a great service. He has made the works, the places and the lives of these surprisingly genial men much more accessible than ever before. In short, he has prised open the sarcophagus of their talent and of their vast store of ghoulish tales. He has also asserted their place at the head of all that was to follow. These talented men, although never entirely forgotten, had been sidelined to some extent by the more famous mainstream Irish novelists. Brian J. Showers has now raised them onto their rightful echelon among the immortals or even, dare I say, among the truly undead.

Pat Liddy
Artane, Dublin

Pat Liddy is author and illustrator of many books and articles on Dublin and is a director of *Pat Liddy's Walking Tours of Dublin*.

INTRODUCTION

Dublin is a ferociously literary city. Visitors are bombarded with memorials to writers such as James Joyce, Oscar Wilde, G.B. Shaw, J.M. Synge and Samuel Beckett on every street corner. Dubliners too are constantly reminded of their literary heritage through announcements of yet another *Ulysses* study group, or Beckett theatre festival. Even the many pubs where they raise their daily pints are likely to boast namesakes of a literary bent.

While these titans of Irish literature are rightfully lauded, there are a number of other native writers who have silently slipped into the shadows of the past. We love a good ghost story, but who was the first to breathe life into the genre? We recognise images of Count Dracula, but who wrote the original novel? We are familiar with the story of Dr Faust's pact with the Devil, but what is Ireland's contribution to the legend? It seems strange that the writers whose fictions delve into universal and supernatural themes such as ghosts, vampires and the Devil go so easily unnoticed.

The guide you hold in your hands is my attempt to reassemble the Dublin of Charles Maturin, Joseph Sheridan Le Fanu and Bram Stoker – Ireland's overlooked scribes of the weird, the horrible and the fantastic.

H.P. Lovecraft observed in his essay *Supernatural Horror in Literature* (1935) that there is, 'a current of weirdness in Irish literature,' and that, 'Ghost and fairy lore have always been of great prominence in Ireland.' Indeed, in the late nineteenth century, Celtic Twilight luminaries such as W.B. Yeats, Lady Gregory and Douglas Hyde 'rediscovered' a rich body of lore populated by banshees, faerie kings and the exploits of such heroes as Cú Chulainn and Fionn Mac Cumhaill. But those indigenous stories, legends and myths, even at their ebb, have always had a profound influence on Irish writers. It may be only appropriate that such a great number of supernatural writers have sprung from Ireland's fertile soil.

Maturin, Le Fanu and Stoker are only three of many. Those who are enthralled by their lives and works will crave more, and I urge them to seek out even more obscure writers in the Irish fantastic and supernatural traditions: Fitz-James O'Brien, Lafcadio Hearn and Lord Dunsany, to name just a few. Their delights and terrors are legion!

A final warning to the curious: If you should ever find yourself with this guide book in hand and the streets of Dublin before you, please consider taking the sites out of order. I gave more thought to biography and chronology than I did to geography and podiatry.

And so I invite you to explore dear, dark Dublin...

Brian J. Showers
Rathmines, Dublin

AUTHOR'S NOTE

Some of the sites listed in this guidebook are privately owned, may have specialised/seasonal hours or necessitate advance booking. Please be respectful of these requirements and all properties mentioned herein.

Also, remember that the churches and cathedrals in this guide are primarily places of worship, not tourist attractions. Actions while in these churches and cathedrals should be conducted with the utmost respect and decorum from believers and non-believers alike.

A few of the sites in these tours are not within easy walking distance of the city centre, although nearly all of them are on the Dublin City Bus line. For up-to-date bus timetables, please see Dublin Bus's webpage: www.dublinbus.ie

I have done my best to make sure that all phone numbers and websites were up-to-date at the time of publication. Still, it is advised that you check with all places mentioned within this guide before visiting them. Many civic museums are closed on Mondays and bank holiday weekends. If you find that something is incorrect or out of date, please contact me at gothicdublin@gmail.com so that future printings can be corrected.

Finally, I would also like to acknowledge the following sources for the use of serveral images. On page 13, the illustration of Charles Maturin is by William Brocas for *New Monthy Magazine* (1819). On page 55, the illustration of Joseph Sheridan Le Fanu is by George Brinsley Le Fanu (1916). And finally on page 95, the photograph of Bram Stoker was taken from *Personal Reminiscences of Henry Irving* (1905).

B.J.S.

On the Pathways of Night
Charles Maturin's Dublin

INTRODUCTION

Is just as true the de'ils in hell
Or Dublin City.

– 'Death and Dr Hornbook', Robert Burns

The Reverend Charles Robert Maturin (1782-1824) spent almost the entire duration of his relatively short forty-two year life in Dublin City. During his lifetime Maturin was known as the eccentric curate of the city centre's largest parish and the author of *Bertram*, a successful play. Despite this reputation, Maturin's acolyte, the poet James Clarence Mangan (1803-1849), wrote, 'Charles Robert Maturin, lived under appreciated – and died unsympathised with, uncared for, unenquired after – and not only forgotten, because he had never been thought about in the first place.'[1]

Maturin was born at the end of the eighteenth century during the height of the gothic literary movement. In his youth he delighted in novels such as Horace Walpole's *The Castle of Otranto* (1764), Ann Radcliffe's *The Mysteries of Udolpho* (1794) and Matthew Lewis's *The Monk* (1796). By the start of his own literary career, his themes and writing style were ensconced in gothic convention and tradition. Despite being a clergyman, Maturin, 'attempted to explore the ground forbidden to man, the sources of visionary terror; "the formless void."' This put him at considerable odds with the Church and set up the quixotic curate for literary obscurity.[2]

Towards the end of the nineteenth century, Maturin accumulated a small cult following that included the likes of Honoré de Balzac (1799-1850)[3], the decadent Charles Baudelaire (1821-1867) and the ubiquitous Oscar Wilde (1854-1900). The book that captivated their imaginations was Maturin's epic gothic novel, *Melmoth the Wanderer* (1820). It was an ingenious new take on the traditional 'pact with the Devil' tale. Today anyone who is familiar with Maturin undoubtedly knows this obscure, post-gothic author for his novel of the damned nomad.

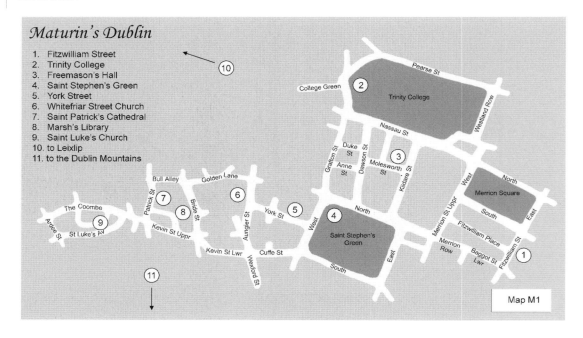

Maturin's Dublin

1. Fitzwilliam Street
2. Trinity College
3. Freemason's Hall
4. Saint Stephen's Green
5. York Street
6. Whitefriar Street Church
7. Saint Patrick's Cathedral
8. Marsh's Library
9. Saint Luke's Church
10. to Leixlip
11. to the Dublin Mountains

Map M1

An 1846 magazine wrote that 'Maturin was an enthusiastic lover of antiquity and had a strange passion for exploring old and desolate houses.'[4] Luckily, enough old and desolate places still exist for us to explore and discover Maturin's – and the Devil's – Dublin.

FITZWILLIAM STREET

If I possess any talent, it is of darkening the gloomy and deepening the sad, of painting life in extremes and representing those struggles of passions when the soul trembles on the verge of the unlawful and the unhallowed.

– from the preface to *The Milesian Chief* (1812)

Charles Robert Maturin was born to William and Fidelia Maturin on 25 September 1782. The exact location of Charles Maturin's birthplace remains unknown, but his parents were listed as living at 8 Fitzwilliam Street in 1806, and, for a long time, this was the family home. Whether this today refers to Fitzwilliam Street Upper or Lower is also unknown, though both houses still stand.

Fitzwilliam Street is a beautiful stretch of Georgian townhouses in the heart of Dublin City. Elegant sash windows, semi-circular fanlights and colourful doors typify the austere Georgian style. The only blemish on Fitzwilliam Street is a massive concrete box that dominates the east side of the street: the offices of Ireland's Electricity Supply Board (ESB). 'In 1963 a total of sixteen structurally sound and complete Georgian houses were destroyed to make space for a sleek new office complex, and in the process the symmetrical Georgian vista was

Fitzwilliam Street

irreparably damaged.'[5] In acknowledgement of their disregard for history and transgression against Dublin's cultural heritage, the ESB bought 29 Fitzwilliam Street Lower and converted it into a period museum. They fully restored the house to what it would have looked like circa 1790-1820, happily for us, a style contemporary with the Fitzwilliam Street of Maturin's time.

While Charles Maturin's father William made a comfortable living working for the Post Office, his grandfather, great-grandfather and great-great-grandfather all served the Church. From an early age, Maturin felt that this would be his calling as well.[6] His literary tastes also developed early as he voraciously read and internalised all the popular gothic novels of the day. Because of his fragile health, Maturin was encouraged by his family to pursue these less strenuous literary endeavours. Tales of gloomy castles, murderous plots of revenge, concealed passages and scenes of dark and stormy nights shaped Maturin's literary tastes. Before long the young Maturin was writing his own short plays and acting them out in the family drawing room.

In later life Maturin, with his firm belief in the Church and his penchant for storytelling, became the embodiment of the best Irish literature. But as Dante, Milton, Marlowe and any storyteller in a pub would tell you, tales about God are not quite as compelling as tales about Old Scratch.

One such story, a favourite told in pubs as far back as Maturin's time, concerns an infernal Black Dog.[7] The story begins with a night-time traveller who, though on his way home from the pub, is no less pious than the local priest. Along a particularly dark stretch of road, the God-fearing traveller encounters a giant hound blocking his way. The hound's coat is as black as the night; red eyes, smoldering with the flames of Hell; and gnashing jaws a-drip with blood. The pious traveller, quivering in his boots with fear, manages only to make the Sign of the Cross. Fortunately, this act is enough to drive the devil-dog away; it vanishes leaving behind noxious fumes of burning sulphur. Presumably the shaken survivor would then hurry back to the pub to tell the tale by the warmth of a crackling fire – and another pint.

If Maturin were indeed exposed to stories like this, he certainly would have assimilated them with relish. In later years, as we shall see, he produced his own tales concerning demonic midnight encounters.

How to Get There

Fitzwilliam Street Lower is the southerly extension of Merrion Square East. The ESB office building is easily spotted as the giant, cement cube on the street's east side. Number 29 (+353 1 702 6165) is at the corner of Fitzwilliam Street Lower and Mount Street Upper.

Fitzwilliam Street Lower is a twenty-minute walk from O'Connell Street Bridge through the meat of central Dublin. Merrion Square Park is a known haunt for black mastiffs, but do not fret, Fitzwilliam Street is only a short sprint from there.

TRINITY COLLEGE

Both Maturin and the fictional John Melmoth attended Trinity College in the heart of Dublin City.[8] Despite his desire to join the theatre, Maturin entered the college in 1795 at the age of fifteen. During his years at Trinity, Maturin began developing the eccentric characteristics for which he would later become known, perhaps compensating for his unrealised dream of becoming an actor. His unusual behaviour at this point, however, was probably considered nothing more than the quirky antics of a typical college student.

Maturin was an excellent student while at Trinity. He was a member of the Historical Society and was often lauded for his 'rhetorical and poetical productions'.[9] He defended gothic literature by developing his own theories on the genre: 'As a medium of excitement or impression, it [terror] was certainly the most powerful that could be used by one human being on another…'[10] Maturin graduated as a classical scholar in 1800. Today, Trinity's library holds few first editions of Maturin's work, although *Melmoth the Wanderer* is now taught in some of the college's English courses.

Trinity College, the *alma mater* of all three writers covered in this guide, is not without its macabre side. While it would be a stretch to say that the college was built on an ancient burial ground, an archaeological excavation in 1999 did uncover numerous post-medieval mass burial pits on campus. The pits were 'densely filled with human and animal bones (including camel)' and were covered with saw marks and other signs of anatomical dissection.[11] Could this be the work of eccentric college students? The site of these grisly mass graves is along the eastern side of the Berkley Library bordering the College Park field.

Not only the site of numerous mass graves, Trinity also holds the distinction of housing Dublin's smallest cemetery.[12] The Chaloner Cemetery is named after Dr Luke Chaloner, the first provost of Trinity, who died in 1613. The cemetery has since been used to inter successive provosts and fellows of the college. The

Trinity College

Chaloner
Cemetery

tiny cemetery is still in use today with the most recent burial in 1994. The steps that descend underneath the chapel are as foreboding as they look. They lead directly into the vaults.

Those who do not wish to spend their afternoon hunting down lost and inconspicuous burial sites within the college, may wish to seek out the Dublin Experience in the Arts Building, a multi-media show that runs through the summer months and details the history of the fair city. (For more on Trinity College, see pages 62 and 102.)

How to Get There

Trinity College is one of Dublin's central landmarks and easy to find. Its main entrance is at the junction of College Green, College Street and Grafton Street, a five-minute walk south from O'Connell Bridge. The Chaloner Cemetery is located at the rear of the Chapel and Dining Hall, near the ATM.

Information on the Dublin Experience and walking tours of the college can be found near the main entrance on College Green.

LISLE HOUSE

After graduating from Trinity, Maturin studied theology and in 1803 became an ordained minister. He immediately took the position of curate at a church in the then remote Loughrea, County Galway. This was his only appointment outside of Dublin. On 7 October of the following year, Maturin married Henrietta Kingsbury, the daughter of Dr Thomas Kingsbury, the Vicar of Kildare.[13] Shortly afterward, in 1806, Maturin was transferred to Saint Peter's Church in Dublin's city centre. Saint Peter's was located in one of Dublin's most well-to-do parishes; the Kingsburys were one of Dublin's oldest and most respected Protestant families. In those days, as in these, it sometimes pays to marry into the right family.

Whilst courting Henrietta, Maturin was a frequent visitor to the Kingsburys' home, then known as Lisle House, at 33 Molesworth Street. Dr Kingsbury had a second daughter named Ann Sarah. Ann Sarah married a man named Charles Elgee and they had a daughter named Jane. Jane married a man named William and had a child whom they named Oscar Fingal O'Flahertie Wills Wilde, making Charles Maturin the great-uncle of our dear Oscar.[14] Wilde would eventually come to surpass Maturin in eccentricity and notoriety, but not without a sly nod of the head to his ancestor. Upon his release from Reading Gaol in 1897, Oscar adopted the *nom de guerre* 'Sebastian Melmoth' until his death in 1900.

Like so many other notable Dublin homes, Lisle House is no longer standing. Molesworth Street, once a stretch of Georgian housing, has mostly been demolished, leaving the street a patchwork of old and new.[15] The faux-Georgian infill that is now number 33 is today still called Lisle House.

One building that did manage to escape the wrecking ball is the Freemasons' Hall on the north side of the street. Presumably the Freemasons' Hall was also 'married into the right family'. The Grand Lodge of Ireland is the second oldest Freemason lodge in the world, dating back to 1725. Its interiors are elaborately designed in a number of different themes, including Egyptian. Tours of the lodge are occasionally offered, even to those who do not know the secret handshake.

At the eastern end of Molesworth Street is Buswell's Hotel and Bar. A plaque outside Buswell's Bar declares it an 'official Dublin pub' and carries the James Joyce seal of approval. Buswell's Bar is also the best place on this tour to observe, first-hand, deal-making devils. Being so close to the Dáil, members of parliament can often be found here having their afternoon pints and crafting agreements affecting national policy. And as we know, deals with the Devil, and those who deal with him, cannot always be trusted; a lesson learned in another Irish pub tale:

A blacksmith is awakened from a restful slumber on a cold winter's night by a firm rapping at the door. On opening the door, he finds a tall man dressed in black from the peak of his hat to the soles of his boots. The man speaks in a low whisper, stating that he is in a dire hurry and that his horse needs to be re-shod. The blacksmith reluctantly accepts only when the man in black promises to pay him well. When the job is complete, the man in black presses a gold guinea into the blacksmith's palm. As the man in black mounts his steed, the blacksmith spies the stranger's feet – not feet, but cloven hooves. The terrified blacksmith is left standing in the dead of night, legs shaking with fear and a lump of iron in the palm of his hand.[16]

From Molesworth Street, proceed to verdant Saint Stephen's Green for a tranquil stroll and a short break from Maturin and the Devil.

How to Get There

Molesworth Street is a short walk halfway down Dawson Street from Trinity's Arts Building/Nassau Street entrance. Unfortunately only a handful of the original houses lining Molesworth Street still remain, including the Freemason's Hall (+353 1 676 1337). Lisle House, which stood on the south side of the street, is sadly no more. Buswell's Hotel and Bar (+ 353 1 614 6500) are at the very end, on the corner of Kildare Street.

SAINT STEPHEN'S GREEN

With his tongue hanging from his lacerated mouth, like that of a baited bull; with one eye torn from the socket, and dangling on his bloody cheek; with a fracture in every limb, and a wound for every pore, he still howled 'life-life-life-mercy!' till a stone, aimed by some pitying hand, struck him down. He fell, trodden in one moment into sanguine and discoloured mud by a thousand feet.

– from *Melmoth the Wanderer* (1820)

The above passage from *Melmoth the Wanderer* is not one most people would associate with a tranquil urban park, but then most people do not know the history of Saint Stephen's Green. For nearly 125 years, Saint Stephen's Green has been the pride of Dublin, a place where visitors go for a peaceful stroll and Dubliners go for a quiet lunch. The main entrance at the top of Grafton Street boasts one of the most photographed structures in Dublin: the Fusilier's Arch, a memorial to those who served in the Second Boer War (1899-1902). The Green's leafy paths and open spaces are speckled with memorials to James Clarence Mangan, W.B. Yeats, Countess Markievicz, Lord Ardilaun and many others. A large ornamental pond, a trademark of the Green's designer William Shepard, spans the northern portion of the park. The Green as it appears today was laid out in 1877 at the sole expense of Arthur Guinness, later Lord Ardilaun, whose statue can now be found on the west side of the Green. The twenty-two acre park was opened to the public three years later, free of charge. If we travel back in time, we find that this was not always the case.

In 1814 the open area that we now know as Saint Stephen's Green was closed to the general public. Those who lived in the houses surrounding the green paid a

above Saint Stephen's Green

below Former site of the gallows on the Green

park tax of one guinea per year in order to gain access, making the park a luxury only afforded by the rich. Private parks in Dublin were not uncommon at that time. In fact, Merrion Square was private until the mid-1970s, while Fitzwilliam Square is private to this day. Saint Stephen's Green was not always a popular attraction, even with the rich, as we will see if we step even further back in time.

During Maturin's lifetime at the beginning of the nineteenth century, many of the houses bordering the Green were vacant, dilapidated or hired out as temporary lodgings. 'The gravel pathways of Saint Stephen's Green were choked with weeds, while the Green itself was denuded of trees.'[17] If we go back further still, we find that the Green has origins of a more sinister nature.

Saint Stephen's Green, laid out in 1662, was part of a larger, sixty-acre plot of marshy common land, used mainly for grazing sheep. A year later the streets surrounding the Green were laid out for residential use. All sides were popular and quickly built upon, save for the west side. One contributing reason was that a gallows pole stood at the south-west corner of the present day Green.[18] For a long time, the area had been used as a place for public executions of the bloodiest kind, a far cry from the pleasantries that we now associate with the park. Not far away was Rapree Fields of which Francis Gerard writes in *Picturesque Dublin Old and New*, 'To pass through this portion of the Green after midnight was a service of danger; for not only was it infested by footpads who would relieve the wanderer of his purse and maybe his life, but he likewise ran the danger of falling into a deep ditch, which was usually a receptacle for the filth of the City.'[19] Just a bit further west of the Green near Lower Mercer Road, stood the church and the attached leper colony after which the Green is named.[20] In the seventeenth century, lepers were not the sort of neighbours that drove up property rates.

While the Green's usage over the years has changed from a marshy paddock to a stage for public execution to a popular tourist attraction, some things never seem to change. By 1671, what is now Grafton Street was described as 'being so foule and out of repaire that persons cannot passe to said Green for the benefit of walks therein.'[21] Today, at the height of the summer season, Grafton Street is so mired with tourists on their way to and from the beautiful Saint Stephen's Green that it is just as difficult to pass down. (For more on Saint Stephen's Green and environs, see page 114.)

How to Get There

Saint Stephen's Green is an easy landmark to find. Its main entrance is at the top of Grafton Street and marked by the Fusilier's Memorial Arch. Dublin Corporation has made navigating the Green easy by installing maps near most of the entrances detailing the park's numerous walks, markers and memorials. And after enjoying the park's many flowered nooks and verdant crannies, you are free to leave, unlike some of the Green's past, less fortunate, visitors.

York Street

He stalked along York Street with an abstracted air, the white scarf and hatband, which he had received, remaining about his beautifully shaped person, and exhibiting to the gaze of the amused and amazed pedestrians whom he literally encountered in his apathy a boot upon one foot and a shoe upon the other.

– James Clarence Mangan on Maturin

Maturin's tenancy at 37 York Street saw both the beginning and the end of his literary career. So as not to compromise his position in the Church, he published under the pseudonym Dennis Jasper Murphy. His first novels, *Fatal Revenge* (1807), *The Wild Irish Boy* (1808) and *The Milesian Chief* (1812), were all second-rate romances. None of these novels brought great success, a reality that was financially devastating to Maturin, who personally funded the publication of the books. And with his paltry church stipend of £80 per annum, Maturin was financially insecure.

Further disaster struck in 1809 when Maturin's father William was dismissed from his position as 'Clerk of the Munster Road' at the post office, for 'malservation' – alleged fraud. The allegations were later disproved and dismissed, but the damage had already been done; damage from which William would never recover. In an effort to support his increasingly financially unstable family, Charles Maturin did two things to supplement his stipend. The first was to tutor university students, a duty at which he excelled but thoroughly abhorred. The second was to start writing professionally, something at which he had not been very successful, but had pursued with passion.

By the time Maturin moved into 37 York Street, he was already known for his extravagant dress and eccentric behaviour. Contributing to his persona as a primitive fop, or proto-dandy, was his extreme predilection for dancing. It is said that Maturin was the first into a quadrille and always the last to leave. Even during the daytime he would darken his drawing room windows and indulge in this delight. Maturin's niece Lady Jane Wilde was also known for peculiar habits of her own. She even adopted her uncle's practice of darkening the drawing room in the middle of the day for the fashionable parties she held at 1 Merrion Square.

Regarding Maturin's third novel, *The Milesian Chief* (1812), an anonymous reviewer wrote of Maturin, 'at some future time [this author will] astonish the public.' This anonymous reviewer turned out to be none other than the Scottish novelist Sir Walter Scott (1771-1832) with whom Maturin began a correspondence in December of 1812. At Scott's suggestion, Maturin sent his first play, *Bertram* (1816), to Lord Byron. Byron liked the play so much that he prompted the play's production at London's Drury Lane Theatre.[22] The celebrated actor Edmund Keane starred, and the play met with overwhelming success. Maturin made £1000, a small fortune in those days.

The remainder of Georgian York Street, demolished winter 2006

Nevertheless, Maturin was a magnet for economic tragedy:

> There is not a shilling I have made by *Bertram* that has not been expended to pay the debts of a scoundrel for whom I had the misfortune to go security, so here I am with scarce a pound in my pocket simpering at any congratulations on having made my fortune.[23]

His two subsequent plays, *Manuel* (1817) and *Fredolfo* (1819), were flops, each running less than a week before closing to bad reviews. But the mentor-protégé relationship between Scott and Maturin continued, even when the latter decided to abandon plays and return to writing novels from the seclusion of his York Street home.

Amidst protest in the 1960s, the majority of York Street was demolished to make room for Dublin Corporation housing and a parking ramp. In the winter of 2006 the last tenants of old York Street, many whose families had lived there for generations, were evicted by the city and the final stretch of Georgian housing was demolished. This time there was no public protest. Number 37 stood on the north side of York Street approximately, near the Royal College of Surgeons main entrance.

But if number 37 were standing today, it might still bear the traces of its previous tenant, who, even in times of economic depression, lived well beyond his means:

The walls of the parlours were done in panels, with scenes from his novels, painted by an artist of some eminence: the richest carpets, ottomans, lustres, and marble tables ornamented the withdrawing-rooms; the most beautiful papers covered the walls, and the ceilings were painted to represent clouds, with eagles in the center, from whose claws depended brilliant lustres.[24]

Maturin's acolyte James Clarence Mangan either worked as a scrivener or lived at 6 York Street, though it is unclear which.[25] For all the comments that Mangan made on Maturin's peculiarities, Mangan had a few quirks of his own:

In addition to the curious little hat...which really resembled the tile that broomstick-riding witches are usually represented with...and little round cloak, he made himself conspicuous by wearing a huge pair of green spectacles...Sometimes, even in the most settled weather, he might be seen parading the streets with a very voluminous umbrella under each arm.[26]

But as any Dubliner will tell you, carrying an umbrella around in sunny and 'settled weather' may not be as crazy as it sounds. In Ireland, there are always rain clouds on the horizon. Mangan was a brilliant poet, though profoundly depressed for the majority of his life. He died of cholera in extreme destitution and loneliness in 1849 at the age of forty-six.

York Street is not without its occult connections. In 1885, W.B. Yeats and George William Russell (Æ) started a lodge on York Street called the Dublin Hermetic Society. Yeats wrote:

A little body of men hired a room on York Street...and began to read papers to one another on the Vedas, the Upanishads, and the Neoplatonists, and on modern mystics and spiritualists. They had no scholarship, and they spoke and wrote badly, but they discussed great problems ardently and simply and unconventionally as men, perhaps, discussed great problems in the medieval universities.

The lodge lasted for one year before being replaced by a branch of Madame Helena Blavatsky's Theosophical Lodge on nearby Ely Street.

Regrettably, Maturin's York Street was no match for the city's overzealous wrecking ball. But if you squint hard enough into the shadows as you pass down the street, you might catch a quick glimpse of the good reverend's ghost, with a boot on one foot and a shoe on the other, accompanied by a quirky man in a tall pointy hat with an umbrella under each arm. Undoubtedly the pair of them are wandering from door to door, a day late for the party.

How to Get There

York Street can be found on the south side of the Royal College of Surgeons, just off Saint Stephen's Green West. At the end of York Street is The Swan Bar (+353 1 475 2722), which is as good a place as any to stop for a pint.

SAINT PETER'S CHURCH

...I wish they would let me do what I am good for, sit down by my magic cauldron,
mix my dark ingredients, see the bubbles work, and the spirits rise, and by the pale
and mystic light, I might show them the 'best of my delights.'

– a letter from Maturin to Sir Walter Scott (2 July 1816)

Not far from Maturin's home, near the intersection of York Street and Aungier
Street, is the former site of Saint Peter's Church, where now stands a YMCA.
During Maturin's time Saint Peter's parish was known for containing 'the most of
the wealth, rank and talents of the metropolis.'[27] Although it is conceivable that
Maturin obtained his position as curate of Saint Peter's through his father-in-law
Dr Kingsbury, his Huguenot ancestry was also probably a contributing factor.
In any case, Maturin held this position from 1806 until his death in 1824, but,
despite his tenure, never rose above the position of curate.

For many years Maturin published under the pseudonym Dennis Jasper
Murphy, as it was deemed improper for a man of the cloth to write the type of
gothic romance that he preferred. Due partly to the natural vanity involved in
taking credit for one's work, Maturin published *Bertram* in 1816 under his own
name and, as a consequence, distanced himself from the Church.[28] However,
this did not stop Maturin from performing his job with vigour and zeal. His
sermons were eloquent, witty and popular with the parishioners. Maturin was as
passionate preaching from the pulpit as he was when writing gothic romances.

Saint Peter's Church has a long and rich history. It is unfortunate that it was
demolished and even more unfortunate that it was replaced by the eyesore that
exists today. The church was built in 1680, closed in 1975 and razed in 1982;
but during its 300-year lifespan, events of much consequence took place within
its walls.

Joseph Sheridan Le Fanu, writer of ghost stories, was married here as was Sir
Thornley Stoker, Bram's brother. Arthur Wellesley, Duke of Wellington (1769-
1852), famous for his exploits against Napoleon at Waterloo, was baptised here
as was the Irish patriot Robert Emmet (1778-1803). The churchyard too had its
fair share of notables. Aside from being where Charles Maturin was first interred,
the yard also received the bodies of Dublin's two most notorious hanging-
judges: John Scott, Lord Clonmel (1739-1798), also known as 'Copper-faced
Jack'; and John Fitzgibbon, Earl of Clare (1749-1802), also known as 'Black
Jack'. The latter of the two judges was not a fan favourite, and is purported to
have said that the Irish people were of no more consequence than stray cats. At
his funeral procession the people of Dublin pelted Fitzgibbon's coffin with mud
and dead cats.[29] Presumably this is an example of Irish wit.

Between 1980 and 1981, the bodies in Saint Peter's churchyard, including
Maturin's, were exhumed – 350 bags and twenty-six caskets – and re-interred
at Saint Luke's in the Coombe, though stray bones were still turning up in the

The Whitefriar
Street Church

YMCA's backlot during a 2003 archaeological excavation. To whom these bones formerly belonged remains uncertain, but speaking of remains:

Next door to the former site of Saint Peter's is the Church of Our Lady of Mount Carmel, otherwise known as the Whitefriar Street Church. This particular church is the little known resting place of a very famous saint, though probably not the saint you would expect. A plaque in an alcove of the church declares an ornate, wooden box to contain the 'sacred body of Saint Valentinus the Martyr, together with a small vessel tinged with his blood.' Saint Valentinus is better known by his Hallmark name, Saint Valentine.[30] The remains of the saint you were expecting, the one with a Dublin cathedral named after him, are said to be in County Down.

How to Get There

Maturin did not have very far to drive to work in the morning. Finding parking must have been much easier in those days too. The former site of Saint Peter's Church is slightly south of the York Street/Aungier Street intersection, where the YMCA now stands. The Whitefriar Street Church (+353 1 475 8821) is also on Aungier Street, slightly north of the aforementioned intersection.

Saint Patrick's Cathedral

The very first sounds almost that attract the ears of childhood are tales of another
life – foolishly are they called tales of superstition; for, however disguised by the
vulgarity of narration, and the distortion of fiction, they tell him of those whom he
is hastening from the threshold of life to join, the inhabitants of the invisible world,
with whom he must soon be, and forever.

– in defense of supernatural tales from *Sermons* (1819)

The Maturin family were historically connected with the Church, and in Dublin
this inevitably leads us to the religious locus of the city, Saint Patrick's Cathedral.
Gabriel Maturin (1640-1718), Charles Maturin's great-great grandfather was a
persecuted Huguenot minister who fled to Ireland from France. Charles Maturin,
whose spry imagination was always ready to embellish a tale, used to spice up
the story somewhat. He often told people that his great-great grandfather was
a foundling on the steps of the orphanage on Rue les Mathurines, and later
made a daring escape to Ireland after spending twenty-six years in the Bastille
for being a Protestant.[31] Maturin's penchant for Gothicism was never fully
satisfied.

Maturin was so influenced by his ancestral connection with the Church
that he believed his family 'remained in service of the church for which [his
great-great grandfather] is alleged to have suffered.'[32] Maturin's grandfather, the
Very Reverend Gabriel James Maturin (1700-1746) was the Dean of Kildare
and later succeeded Jonathan Swift as Dean of Saint Patrick's in 1745. Quick
math will reveal that Gabriel James Maturin was Dean of Saint Patrick's for less
than a year before he died. However, his short time as Dean of Saint Patrick's
earned him distinguished burial rights, and his remains were placed beneath
the communion table traditionally used by the Huguenots in Saint Patrick's Lady
Chapel. Aside from church records, there is no memorial marking his burial.

Numerous churches have existed on the site of Saint Patrick's since 405 AD.
The present structure was erected between approximately 1220 and 1254,
with the tower added after a fire in 1362. The site was chosen for its proximity
to the legendary well where tradition holds that Saint Patrick first baptised
and converted the heathen Irish to Christianity. Most legends seem to have an
element of truth in them; indeed during a 1901 archaeological excavation an
ancient well was discovered at the cathedral's north-west corner. Two Celtic
grave slabs decorated with early Christian symbols were unearthed nearby. The
two slabs are now on display within the cathedral. A plaque erected over the
well, near the cathedral's western park entrance, reads:

Near here is the reputed site of the well
where St. Patrick baptised many of the local inhabitants
in the fifth century AD.

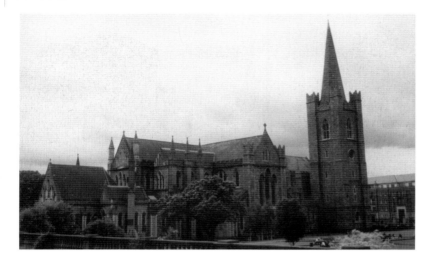

Saint Patrick's Cathedral borders Dublin's Liberties district, known historically as the city's poorest neighbourhood. The cathedral was not always in as fine a shape as it is today. In the early nineteenth century, the cathedral's garden was filled with shacks and lean-tos brimming with the poor. Sir Benjamin Lee Guinness restored the cathedral between 1860 and 1865. It was then that the handsome Saint Patrick's Park was laid out on the cathedral's north side. At the eastern end of the park is the Dublin Millennium Literary Parade funded by Jameson Irish Whiskey and erected in 1988. The wall includes memorials to Jonathan Swift, Eilís Dillon, James Clarence Mangan, Oscar Wilde, W.B. Yeats, John Millington Synge, Sean O'Casey, James Joyce, Brendan Behan, Austin Clarke and Samuel Beckett. Among them are three Nobel Prize winners for literature. Try and guess which.

The cathedral's most famous dean was, of course, Jonathan Swift (1667-1745). Inside the cathedral are the remains of Dean Swift and his adored Esther Johnson (1681-1728), better known as 'Stella'. Also in the cathedral is a small Swift exhibit that includes everything from first editions to a cast of Swift's skull made at the time of his death.[33] A memorial plaque to Dean Swift reads:

> Here is laid the body of Jonathan Swift, Doctor of Divinity, Dean of this Cathedral Church, where fierce indignation can no longer rend the heart. Go, traveller, and imitate if you can this earnest and dedicated champion of liberty. He died on the 19th day of October 1745 AD. Aged 78 years.

Saint Patrick's Cathedral is one of Dublin's finest landmarks and should be on every sightseer's list. Many memorials line the walls of the cathedral, including a massive monument to Narcissus Marsh, former Archbishop of Dublin (1638-1713). Jonathan Swift moved the oversized memorial inside the cathedral from the churchyard. It is true that Swift was a very powerful man in eighteenth-century Dublin, but he most likely had help when moving the Marsh monument.

Saint Patrick's Park

How to Get There

Saint Patrick's Cathedral (+353 1 453 9472) is a stone's throw away from Saint Peter's Church, only a couple of blocks westward. The most impressive view of the cathedral is when it is approached from Golden Lane. From the intersection of Aungier Street and York Street, walk north on Aungier Street taking the first left onto Golden Lane, the first intersection north of York Street. A short walk west will bring you to Saint Patrick's Cathedral.

Bas-reliefs of the most memorable scenes from *Travels Into Several Remote Nations Of The World. In Four Parts. by Lemuel Gulliver, First a Surgeon, and then a Captain of several Ships.* (1726), more commonly known as *Gulliver's Travels*, decorate the modern apartment block on the corner of Golden Lane and Bride Street just opposite the church.

MARSH'S LIBRARY

During his lifetime, Maturin was a frequent visitor to Marsh's Library, which lies in the churchyard immediately adjacent to Saint Patrick's Cathedral. William Carleton (1794-1864) wrote in his autobiography that 'Maturin had not only been a reader [in Marsh's] but wrote the greater portion of several of his novels on a small plain deal desk which he moved from place to place according as it suited his privacy or convenience.'[34] This was not Maturin's only peculiar writing habit.

Maturin supposedly wrote the entirety of *Melmoth the Wanderer* in the stillness of the night for fear of disruption and losing his muse. Even stranger still is the story that, Maturin would paste a wafer to his forehead, or paint his face with phosphorous when writing. This was a warning to those around him that he was in the midst of composition, and that he was not to be disturbed.

far left Marsh's Library

left The interior of
Marsh's Library
(courtesy of Marsh's Library)

Charles Maturin was not the last of the family to be associated with Marsh's Library. His son, Reverend William Maturin (1807-1887), was appointed Keeper of the library in 1872 through the influence of Sir William Wilde. William Maturin remained Keeper at Marsh's until his death in 1887. A photograph of him is still occasionally on display in the library. Marsh's holds copies of works by both Maturins: including first editions of Charles Maturin's sermons, but, like Trinity College, the library possesses no other first editions of his work.

Archbishop Marsh built the library in 1701.[35] The first Keeper was Dr Elias Bouhéreau, a Huguenot refugee from France like Gabriel Maturin. The present Keeper, Dr Murial McCarthy, is proud to say that, though just over three hundred years old, Marsh's is a functioning library to this day. The collection is comprised of nearly 25,000 volumes on subjects that range as widely as theology, classical literature, navigation and medicine.

When the library was built, books were still a luxury of the rich, making the idea of a public library fairly novel. Interesting precautions taken to prevent theft included chaining books to shelves and the rather inventive 'reading cages'. Readers were locked into cages with the books they wanted to read. When finished, the reader would ring a small bell, and a librarian would let them out. Visitors leaving the building were always searched.

Marsh's Library, like any good library, is haunted. Some believe the ghost is that of Archbishop Marsh. Before eloping with a sea captain, the archbishop's niece, Grace Marsh, was said to have left a letter of apology in one of the books. He now roams the library each night searching the volumes for the letter from his estranged niece. In a strange twist to the story, Grace Marsh was buried in Saint Patrick's churchyard, in the very same grave as her uncle.

Others believe that the ghost is none other than Dean Swift, who was known to frequent the library.[36] Many books in the library still bear his oft-inflammatory notes scribbled in the margins. However, the ghost could always be that of some restless and tormented librarian who wanders the halls still hoping to collect overdue book fines.

How to Get There

Marsh's Library (+353 1 454 3511), and its reader cages, is on Saint Patrick's Close on the south side of the Saint Patrick's Cathedral.

SAINT LUKE'S CHURCH

[Ireland] is bleeding under ignorance, poverty, and superstition, and we cast over its wounds gay embroidered garments of voluptuousness, beneath which the heavings and shudderings of its agony are but more frightfully visible.

– from *The Wild Irish Boy* (1808)

Toward the end of his days, Maturin's health started to falter. Little is actually known of his personal life as he withdrew deeper into the seclusion of his York Street home. He was working in what we would now call a dead-end job, his literary failures outnumbered his successes and, in 1821, he and his wife Henrietta lost a child in childbirth.[37] Mangan described Maturin's disconsolate state after the latter officiated a funeral:

His long, pale, melancholy, Don Quixote, out-of-the-world face would have inclined you to believe that Dante, Bajazet and the Cid had risen together from their sepulchers, and clubbed their features for the production of the effect. But...the great Irishman, like Hamlet, had that within him much passed show...he bore the 'thunder-scars' about him, but they were graven not on his brow, but on his heart.

The final blow came in October of 1824 when Maturin came down with 'an acute malady that impaired his health in general.'[38] Maturin finally succumbed on 30 October 1824. A persistent belief is that Maturin took his own life with an overdose of laudanum, or even that the overdose was an accidental poisoning, but neither story is substantiated. Maturin was interred at Saint Peter's Church on 2 November, a heartbreaking ending for 'a warm and kind-hearted man' who had a penchant for dancing, merriment and a zest for life.[39]

Before Saint Peter's Church was demolished in 1985, the bodies in the vaults and churchyard were exhumed and re-interred at Saint Luke's in the Coombe. The remains, all unmarked due to an earlier removal of the gravestones and memorials, consisted of 350 bags and twenty-six caskets. Maturin's remains were presumably among them.

Saint Luke's as it now stands is in extreme disrepair. It was closed in 1975 and used as church offices until 1981. The church's ancient frame was further victimised in the mid-1980s when hooligans savagely torched the roof, damaging their neighbourhood's cultural heritage. The hollow, blackish-gray hull, now owned by the city, stands vacant on a small hill rising over Weaver Street.

Saint Luke's in the Coombe

There is a story about the Devil told in reference to many churches speckled throughout Dublin and, by the looks of the ruins, it may also apply to Saint Luke's. Various Dublin churches are known locally as the 'Black Church'. Two such examples being the Chapel of Ease on Saint Mary's Street on the north side and (see page 57) the Holy Trinity Church on Church Avenue in Rathmines. Like the moniker, the local legend is always consistent: anyone who walks widdershins around the church at midnight will summon the Devil himself for a private audience. The fact that there are no reports of this actually working by no means implies that the story is untrue.

Maturin's body was originally buried in the yard of one of Dublin's richest churches and later moved to one of the city's most impoverished. Saint Luke's was built in 1708 in a parish that has always been known for its extreme poverty. An eighteenth-century annual charity event claimed Saint Luke's to be 'The poorest Parish in Dublin.'[40] The Coombe and the surrounding Liberties district have been known for their poverty for centuries, and today they are known for an acute drug problem as well. Of course the area is not without its charm.

The Coombe area and its environs are the oldest part of the city, originally settled by the Vikings in 1088. The area is now filled with many who have lived there their entire lives, like their parents before them and so on, giving the neighbourhood a strong sense of identity and community. Considering the level of crime that exists in the area by night, you will not find a friendlier neighbourhood by day. Maturin may have been right when he wrote:

> I believe [Ireland] the only country on earth, where, from the strange existing opposition of religion, politics, and matter, the extremes of refinement and barbarism are united, and the most wild and incredible of romantic stories are hourly passing before modern eyes.[41]

Another interesting feature of the Coombe is its Liberty Market whose slogan is 'Why pay shop price?' The market, located on Meath Street, is in what looks to be a covered alley composed of wire cage stalls where vendors sell everything from cheap bed dressings to cheap books to cheap jewelry. An interesting place to browse, you may even find a good deal. After all, why should you pay shop price?

While the Coombe may seem innocent enough during the day, I feel it is my duty to warn against lingering for too long, too far from main roads or too late into the night. And always make sure you are walking clock-wise around any church you encounter. We do not want any accidents.

How to Get There

From Saint Patrick's Cathedral, the Coombe is best reached via Dean Street. Saint Luke's is best viewed from Weaver Street, the first left off the Coombe. The Liberty Market is about midway up Meath Street on the right. The Liberties district is still known for its poverty and, in this modern day, its drug problem. It is ill advised to wander too far, especially if you look like a tourist or James Clarence Mangan.

LEIXLIP CASTLE

> The Castle of Leixlip, at that period, possessed a character of romantic beauty and feudal grandeur, such as few buildings in Ireland can claim – Leixlip, though about seven miles from Dublin, has all the sequestered and picturesque character that imagination could ascribe to a landscape a hundred miles from, not only the metropolis, but an inhabited town.
>
> – from 'Leixlip Castle' (1825)

On the Leixlip main road, just past the bridge over the Rye Water, is a tall, iron-gate to a walled estate. Through the gate and down the path lies a beautiful, medieval castle near where the Rye Water and Liffey River meet. The castle, known as Leixlip Castle, has been in the care of the Honourable Desmond Guinness since 1958.[42] While Mr Guinness owns the castle today, Charles Maturin, for however small a fraction, lays claim to a part of the castle's

Leixlip Castle

imagined history. His short story 'Leixlip Castle' was first published in 1825.

In his only known short story, Maturin created a sinister history for the castle, the history of the unfortunate Sir Redmond Blaney and the fate of his three daughters; a history in which devilry plays an inevitable role.

The tale begins with the misfortune of Sir Redmond's youngest daughter Jane. Young Jane had been playing 'far and deep' in the castle's surrounding woods with the daughter of a servant. Jane's playmate returned alone at nightfall, weeping:

> Her account was, that, in passing through a lane at some distance from the castle, an old woman...suddenly started out of the thicket and took Jane Blaney by the arm. She had in her hand two rushes, one of which she threw over her shoulder, and giving the other to the child, motioned her to do the same. Her young companion, terrified at what she saw, was running away, when Jane Blaney called after her – 'Good-bye, good-bye, it is a long time before you will see me again.'

The forests were searched and ponds drained, but her body was never found. An even ghastlier fate befell Sir Redmond's eldest daughter on her wedding night:

> The marriage was celebrated at the Castle of Leixlip; and, after the bride and bridegroom had retired, the guests still remained drinking to their future happiness, when suddenly, to the great alarm of Sir Redmond and his friends, loud and piercing cries were heard to issue from the part of the castle in which the bridal chamber was situated.
>
> Some of the more courageous hurried upstairs; it was too late – the wretched bridegroom had burst, on that fatal night, into a sudden and most horrible paroxyism

The Wonderful Barn

of insanity. The mangled form of the unfortunate and expiring lady bore attestation to the mortal virulence with which the disease had operated on the wretched husband, who died a victim to it himself after the involuntary murder of his bride. The bodies were interred as soon as decency would permit, and the story hushed up.

Poor Sir Redmond, with one daughter left, did what any sane father would do – he put her in the care of a withered, witch-like crone who had been nurse to the late Lady Blaney. The old hag, 'whose memory was a complete *Thesaurus terrorum*,' tainted the poor child with stories of magic and witchcraft. And what happened next is perhaps the weirdest incident of all. The full story can be found on page 43.

The real history of the castle is every bit as exciting as Maturin's fictional account. The Danes, who called Leixlip *'lax-hlaup'*, or Salmon's Leap, first settled the area. It is unclear when the castle was originally built, but most speculations place it about the twelfth century. The castle and town were both attacked by the King of Scotland, Robert the Bruce in 1317. His company, 'burnt part of the towne, [and] brake down the church and spoiled it.'[43] Fortunately the town and church were rebuilt and Leixlip became the pleasant small town suburb that it is today.

Perhaps a highpoint in Leixlip's history is when two brothers started a small brewery on the banks of the Liffey near the main bridge into town. A small plaque was erected to commemorate the event:

Arthur and Richard Guinness leased a brewery here in 1756

35

Those who spend the day in Leixlip, after a carvery lunch at Darkie Moore's comfortable restaurant and lounge, may wish to seek out the two local curiosities. The Conolly family of Castletown, in an effort to employ the poor during a particularly harsh winter in the mid-1740s, funded two relief projects. The first is now known as 'The Wonderful Barn' and is indeed a wonderful sight. The structure is conical in shape and speckled with numerous small, triangular windows. The oddest feature of the barn is a staircase that winds up the structure around the outside of the wall.

The second structure is known locally as the 'Obelisk', or 'Conolly's Folly'. This structure is best described as an observation tower, though also would bear resemblance to a multi-arched chimney, if such a thing existed. The Obelisk is in poor shape and ascending its arches is ill advised, if not illegal.

A little closer to Leixlip are the Rye Water and Liffey River walks, two short trails that follow the aforementioned rivers. The trails begin just off the main road in Leixlip and can be quite pleasant all year round.

How to Get There

The easiest way to Leixlip is by taking a bus from the city centre (please check with Dublin Bus for details). The Western Suburban train line also stops at the two Leixlip stations. The Western Suburban line can be taken from Connolly Station in the city centre.

Leixlip Castle and the adjacent grounds are private property and should be treated as such. Public tours of the castle are offered seasonally. Please check with the Leixlip Town Council for details (www.kildare.ie/leixlip).

The gates to Leixlip Castle are on the main road near Darkie Moore's Restaurant and the Rye Water Bridge. The Rye Water and Liffey River walks start across the street from Darkie Moore's, and are particularly nice in the spring. The Wonderful Barn is a bit south of Leixlip in a field just off Celbridge Road, about one and a half kilometres (nearly one mile) from the main road. The Obelisk, far out of walking distance, lies between Leixlip and Maynooth. While there are no signs specifically stating 'No Trespassing', the Wonderful Barn and Obselisk are on private property. One should keep this in mind when taking a quick, unobtrusive peek at these wonderful buildings.

THE HELL-FIRE CLUB LODGE

> At this moment is there one of us present, however we may have departed from the Lord, disobeyed his will, and disregarded his word – is there one of us who would, at this moment, accept all that man could bestow, or earth afford, to resign the hope of salvation? – No, there is not one – not such a fool on earth, were the enemy of mankind to traverse it with the offer!
>
> – from *Sermons* (1819)

Maturin's most famous work, the one for which his name is remembered when remembered at all, is *Melmoth the Wanderer* (1820). The novel is a disjointed epic narrative of stories within stories, that lies somewhere between conventional gothic horror and religious satire. Melmoth the Wanderer sold his soul to the Devil for knowledge and extended life. When the contract expires, his soul will be eternally damned. The Wanderer roams the earth in search of a soul in a more wretched condition than his, a soul who would willingly and knowingly take over the contract. The Wanderer's history evolves through a series of second hand narratives, beginning in typical gothic fashion with the Wanderer's scion John Melmoth approaching Melmoth Lodge in the Wicklow Mountains to tend to his miserly uncle on his death-bed:

> The lodge was in ruins, and a barefooted boy from an adjacent cabin ran to lift on its single hinge what had once been a gate, but was now a few planks so villainously put together, that they clattered like a sign in a high wind. The stubborn post of the gate, yielding at last to the united strength of John and his barefooted assistant, grated heavily through the mud and gravel stones, in which it left a deep and sloughy furrow, and the entrance lay open.

John finds his uncle in bed surrounded by servants. Paranoid and avaricious to the very end, Old Melmoth does not trust the servants. He bids his nephew to fetch a glass of wine from his private study, where John spies the object of his uncle's, soon his own, obsession:

> There was a great deal of decayed and useless lumber, such as might be supposed to be heaped up to a miser's closet; but John's eyes were in a moment, and as if by magic, rivetted on a portrait that hung on the wall....from an impulse equally resistless and painful, he approached the portrait, held the candle towards it, and could distinguish the words on the border of the painting, – Jno. Melmoth, anno 1646.[44]

In a state of pure terror and fright, 'Old Melmoth...died as he had lived, in a kind of avaricious delirium.' Old Melmoth's will and last testament stipulates that his nephew remove and destroy the portrait of their cursed ancestor, the Wanderer. Furthermore, the will bids John to destroy a manuscript that accompanies the portrait. Before carrying out his uncle's will, John reads the manuscript, an account written by a mad Englishman named Stanton.

Stanton first encountered the enigmatic Wanderer in Valencia, Spain where his own obsession begins at an ill-fated wedding party. The priest presiding over the wedding recognises the uninvited Wanderer and, like Old Melmoth, dies of fright. Stanton encounters the immortal Wanderer a second time in London where he approaches him. The Wanderer, with his infernal knowledge of the future, tells Stanton when they will next meet: 'the place shall be the bare walls of a mad-house, where you shall rise rattling in your chains, and rustling from your straw, to greet me – yet still you shall have the *curse of sanity*. I *never desert my friends in misfortune*. When they are plunged in the lowest abyss of human calamity, *they are sure to be visited by me*.'

Through a sequence of events that can only be found in sprawling gothic narratives, Stanton sinks into the squalor of a mad-house where he is eventually visited by Melmoth the Wanderer:

> You must be content with the spider and the rat, to crawl and scratch round your flock-bed! I have known prisoners in the Bastile to feed them for companions...I have known a spider to descend at the tap of a finger, and a rat to come forth when the daily meal was brought, to share it with his fellow-prisoner! – How delightful to have vermin for your guests! Aye, and when the feast fails them, they make a meal of their entertainer! – You shudder – Are you, then, the first prisoner who has been devoured alive by vermin that infested his cell?...Your guests, however, will give you one token of repentance while they feed; there will be *gnashing of teeth*!

Stanton is indeed in the lowest abyss of human calamity. Melmoth the Wanderer's true purpose becomes clear when he offers Stanton a deal. The Wanderer will relieve Stanton of his pathetic position if he willingly trades places. Stanton would acquire infernal foreknowledge and an unnatural life span though at the cost of his own soul:

The Hell-Fire Lodge's hearth

'Escape – escape for your life,' cried the tempter; 'break forth into life, liberty and sanity. Your social happiness, your intellectual powers, your immortal interests, perhaps, depend on the choice of this moment. – There is the door, and the key is my hand. Choose – choose!'

Stanton is a God-fearing, Christian soul and, despite his earthly position, rejects Melmoth's infernal offer. 'Begone, monster, demon! – begone to your native place. Even this mansion of horror trembles to contain you; its walls sweat, and its floors quiver, while you tread on them.' And so the Wanderer continues to roam the earth, searching for the miserable soul who would switch places with him. The novel's climax takes place where it begins – on a dark and stormy night at Melmoth Lodge, which, dear reader, you need but a library card to discover.

Maturin found inspiration for his stories on his frequent walks in the Dublin and Wicklow Mountains. The Hell-Fire Club Lodge on Mount Pelier Hill (sometimes written Montpelier) in the Dublin Mountains, bears more than a passing resemblance to stoic and hell-haunted Melmoth Lodge. And the Hell-Fire Lodge's dark history easily contends with its fictional counterpart. Maturin, describing Melmoth Lodge, simultaneously describes the Hell-Fire Lodge:

There was not fence or a hedge round the domain: an uncemented wall of loose stones, whose numerous gaps were filled with furze or thorns, supplied their place. There was not a tree or a shrub on the lawn; the lawn itself was turned into pasture-ground, and a few sheep were picking their scanty food amid the pebble stones, thistles, and hard mould, through which a few blades of grass made their rare and squalid appearance.

The lodge, sometimes known as 'The Devil's Kitchen', always seems to have been in ruins, and had been for nearly fifty years before Maturin had ever been born. The Right Honourable William Conolly of Castletown, of the same Conolly

family responsible for the two wonderful follies of Leixlip, built the structure as a summer hunting lodge around 1725. What stood atop the hill before the lodge may be accountable for the lodge's tumultuous history. A sacred stone cairn, pre-historic in construction, was destroyed and used as building material.

The first sign of trouble came shortly after the lodge was erected, when a raging storm blew the slated-roof off. This was thought to be the Devil's retaliation for desecrating the pagan cairn. Conolly responded by rebuilding a roof of stone, which has yet to be demolished by the Devil and can still be seen to this day. But the real trouble did not begin until the lodge came into use by Dublin's notorious Hell-Fire Club. [45]

Richard Parsons, Earl of Rosse and Colonel Jack St Leger founded the Dublin Hell-Fire Club around 1735. Members of the club were rakes; very rich and very bored men of genteel upbringing. They alleviated this boredom by acting in outrageous, offensive, and dangerous ways. Their headquarters was at the Eagle Tavern on Cork Hill near Dublin Castle. They would meet there to drink and gamble. They drank a potent beverage called *scaltheen* made from Irish whiskey and melted butter. During these meetings they would sometimes catch a cat, soak the poor creature in *scaltheen* and set it alight, letting it escape, flaming and yowling into the streets. The club's boisterous and dangerous exploits turned more sinister when they decided to toast the Devil, dabble in satanic magic and perform black masses. [46]

The Club rented Conolly's hunting lodge where they would be free to revel in their blasphemous past times. The lodge became the site of drunken orgies, satanic rituals and black magic. A famous story about the club concerns a simple, high-stakes card game. Presumably this was an off-night – no drunken orgies or black rituals. As they played, a stranger seeking refuge from the raging storm outside knocked upon the door of the lodge. Angelic as hosts, the club members asked the stranger inside. The stranger took a seat by the fire and was soon invited to join the game. The spirits flowed and eventually the gamblers, in an attempt to shock one another and liven-up the game, started betting their souls. With all their souls on the table, the players slowly revealed their cards. Much to their dismay, the stranger won. That's when they noticed the stranger had cloven hooves where he should have had feet.

The blasphemous revelries of the first Hell-Fire Club lasted until about 1740 when one of the club's most notorious members, Richard 'Burn-Chapel' Whaley, set the lodge on fire. The club retained a young child, who lived in the Kilakee House at the base of the hill, as a servant and pint-sized barkeep. The story goes that the child spilled whiskey on Burn-Chapel Whaley's coat, provoking his incendiary wrath. Whaley lit the child on fire, who in turn lit the drapes and other inflammables as he ran about the lodge screaming. Soon the whole lodge was engulfed in flames, burning alive those too drunk to escape. The lodge has stood vacant ever since. To add credence to the story, workers found an unmarked grave while renovating the Kilakee House in 1970. The grave contained the remains of a small child.[47]

Not surprisingly, stories of a large black cat that stalks the hill are also associated with the lodge, harking back to the old Irish pub tale. Stories of this nature have persisted for nearly two centuries though it is only in recent years that the animal shelter moved to nearby Stocking Lane. Any sightings before that were most likely the Devil himself in feline form.

The lodge still stands atop Mount Pelier today. By day, picnickers make use of the hill and surrounding woods. By night, teenagers and, some say, witch covens use the area for festivities similar to those held in days of yore. The stone roof is still completely intact and the dark rooms, blackened by soot, can easily be explored. The fireplaces are still set into the walls though it is unknown at which hearth the dark stranger warmed his hooves. Near one of the fireplaces a vandal has scrawled on the wall 'No one can leave here.' One wonders if Maturin himself was ever drawn to the lodge and its sinister past – if he ever explored the charred rooms or spied the ghost of the child-servant haunting the hall. If he had, he certainly infused traces of Dublin's most haunted locale into the memorable classic, *Melmoth the Wanderer.*

How to Get There

There is no easy way to the Hell-Fire Club lodge unless you have access to a car. Those without a car can take a bus from the city centre to Ballyboden Road. From there you will have to walk nearly four kilometers (two and a half miles) south on Stocking Lane and Kilakee Road. There is precious little shoulder along the road to the Lodge, so exercise extreme caution when venturing there on foot. Stocking Lane turns into Kilakee Road. After nearly one kilometre (just over half a mile) on Kilakee Road, and just after Massey's Woods, you will come to a public car park and a sign that reads 'Hell-Fire Woods'. From the car park you will find the path to the lodge, an exceedingly steep incline lined with rocks and thistle. From there, dear traveller, you are on your own.

Epilogue

Those meeting Charles Maturin for the first time expected to find a man who was a reflection of the novels he wrote – shrouded in darkness, gloom and Gothicism. Instead they found the opposite – 'the gayest of the gay, passionately fond of society.'[48] Maturin, typically clad in bright colours, always enjoyed a good party and was known to continue dancing long after the others had stopped. Mangan later pointed out that addictions were often caused by depression, which he himself was profoundly familiar with. 'Some men turn to drink,' he said, '[Maturin] who was always less conventional, turned to dance.' And so Maturin lived his life, always dancing to keep the world at bay; pursuing his passion for writing until the very end.

Melmoth the Wanderer, a tale of a damned anti-hero's powerless efforts to correct his mistakes, reflects not only Maturin's helpless wanderings through the literary world, but also the underlying theme that we live in the Hell we create. We are responsible for our own position in life. Much to his dismay, and perhaps guilt, the outdated gothic romances that Maturin chose to write were not terribly popular during his lifetime. It was not until the end of the Victorian era, when Gothic themes were briefly revisited, that Maturin found brief popularity, but it was not long before he was again forgotten.

Maturin's remains, like Melmoth, have restlessly wandered, from Saint Peter's on Aungier Street to Saint Luke's in the Coombe. The latter church has been earmarked by the Dublin City Council as a cultural heritage site and is slated for renovations. The bodies in the vaults will again be disinterred and relocated to another place even further out of sight and, mostly likely, out of memory. I leave the final memory to Maturin's close friend, James Clarence Mangan:

> The third and last time that I beheld this marvelous man I remember well. It was some time before his death, on a balmy autumn evening, in 1824. He slowly descended the steps of his own house...and took his way in the direction of Whitefriars Street, in Castle Street, and passed the Royal Exchange into Dame Street, every second person staring at him and the extraordinary double-belted, treble-caped rug of an old garment – neither coat nor cloak – which enveloped his person....[I]nstead of passing along Dame Street, where he would have been 'the observed of all observers,' he wended his way along the dark and forlorn locality of Dame Lane, and having reached the end of this not very classical thoroughfare, crossed over to Angelsea, where I lost sight of him...I never saw him afterwards.
>
> – James Clarence Mangan on Maturin

LEIXLIP CASTLE:
AN IRISH FAMILY LEGEND

by Charles Maturin

The incidents of the following tale are not merely founded on fact, they are facts themselves, which occurred at no very distant period in my own family. The marriage of the parties, their sudden and mysterious separation, and their total alienation from each other until the last period of their mortal existence, are all facts. I cannot vouch for the truth of the supernatural solution given to all these mysteries; but I must still consider the story as a fine specimen of Gothic horrors, and can never forget the impression it made on me when I heard it related for the first time among many other thrilling traditions of the same description.

C.R.M.

The tranquillity of the Catholics of Ireland during the disturbed periods of 1715 and 1745, was most commendable, and somewhat extraordinary; to enter into an analysis of their probable motives, is not at all the object of the writer of this tale, as it is pleasanter to state the fact of their honour, than at this distance of time to assign dubious and unsatisfactory reasons for it. Many of them, however, showed a kind of secret disgust at the existing state of affairs, by quitting their family residences and wandering about like persons who were uncertain of their homes, or possibly expecting better from some near and fortunate contingency.

Among the rest was a Jacobite Baronet, who, sick of his uncongenial situation in a Whig neighbourhood, in the north – where he heard of nothing but the heroic defence of Londonderry; the barbarities of the French generals; and the resistless exhortations of the godly Mr Walker, a Presbyterian clergyman, to whom the citizens gave the title of 'Evangelist'; – quitted his paternal residence, and about the year 1720 hired the Castle of Leixlip for three years (it was then the property of the Connollys, who let it to triennial tenants); and removed thither with his family, which consisted of three daughters – their mother having long been dead.

The Castle of Leixlip, at that period, possessed a character of romantic beauty and feudal grandeur, such as few buildings in Ireland can claim, and which is now, alas, totally effaced by the destruction of its noble woods; on the destroyers of which the writer would wish 'a minstrel's malison were said'. – Leixlip, though about seven miles from Dublin, has all the sequestered and picturesque character that imagination could ascribe to a landscape a hundred miles from, not only the metropolis but an inhabited town. After driving a dull mile (an Irish mile) in passing from Lucan to Leixlip, the road – hedged up on one side of the high wall that bounds the demesne of the Veseys, and on the other by low enclosures, over whose rugged tops you have no view at all – at once opens on Leixlip Bridge, at almost a right angle, and displays a luxury of landscape on which the eye that has seen it even in childhood dwells with delighted recollection. – Leixlip Bridge, a rude but solid structure, projects from a high bank of the Liffey, and slopes rapidly to the opposite side, which there lies remarkably low. To the right the plantations of the Vesey's demesne – no longer obscured by walls – almost mingle their dark woods in its stream, with the opposite ones of Marshfield and St Catherine's. The river is scarcely visible, overshadowed as it is by the deep, rich and bending foliage of the trees. To the left it bursts out in all the brilliancy of light, washes the garden steps of the houses of Leixlip, wanders round the low walls of its churchyard, plays, with the pleasure-boat moored under the arches on which the summer-house of the Castle is raised, and then loses itself among the rich woods that once skirted those grounds to its very brink. The contrast on the other side, with the luxuriant walks, scattered shrubberies, temples seated on pinnacles, and thickets that conceal from you the sight of the river until you are on its banks, that mark the character of the grounds which are now the property of Colonel Marly, is peculiarly striking.

Visible above the highest roofs of the town, though a quarter of a mile distant from them, are the ruins of Confy Castle, a right good old predatory tower of the stirring times when blood was shed like water; and as you pass the bridge you catch a glimpse of the waterfall (or salmon-leap, as it is called) on whose noon-day lustre, or moon-light beauty, probably the rough livers of that age when Confy Castle was 'a tower of strength', never glanced an eye or cast a thought, as they clattered in their harness over Leixlip Bridge, or waded through the stream before that convenience was in existence.

Whether the solitude in which he lived contributed to tranquillise Sir Redmond Blaney's feelings, or whether they had begun to rust from want of collision with those of others, it is impossible to say, but certain it is, that the good Baronet began gradually to lose his tenacity in political matters; and except when a Jacobite friend came to dine with him, and drink with many a significant 'nod and beck and smile', the King over the water – or the parish-priest (good man) spoke of the hopes of better times, and the final success of the *right* cause, and the old religion – or a Jacobite servant was heard in the solitude of the large mansion whistling "Charlie is my darling", to which Sir Redmond involuntarily responded in a deep bass voice, somewhat the worse for wear, and marked with more emphasis than good discretion – except, as I have said, on such occasions, the Baronet's politics, like his life, seemed passing away without notice or effort. Domestic calamities, too, pressed sorely on the old gentleman: of his three daughters the youngest, Jane, had disappeared in so extraordinary a manner in her childhood, that though it is but a wild, remote family tradition, I cannot help relating it:

The girl was of uncommon beauty and intelligence, and was suffered to wander about the neighbourhood of the castle with the daughter of a servant, who was also called Jane, as a *nom de caresse*. One evening Jane Blaney and

'Cold – cold – cold how long it is since I have felt a fire!'

her young companion went far and deep into the woods; their absence created no uneasiness at the time, as these excursions were by no means unusual, till her playfellow returned home alone and weeping, at a very late hour. Her account was, that, in passing through a lane at some distance from the castle, an old woman, in the *Fingallian* dress, (a red petticoat and a long green jacket), suddenly started out of a thicket, and took Jane Blaney by the arm: she had in her hand two rushes, one of which she threw over her shoulder, and giving the other to the child, motioned to her to do the same. Her young companion, terrified at what she saw, was running away, when Jane Blaney called after her – 'Good-bye, good-bye, it is a long time before you will see me again.' The girl said they then disappeared, and she found her way home as she could. An indefatigable search was immediately commenced – woods were traversed, thickets were explored, ponds were drained – all in vain. The pursuit and the hope were at length given up. Ten years afterwards, the housekeeper of Sir Redmond, having remembered that she left the key of a closet where sweetmeats were kept, on the kitchen table, returned to fetch it. As she approached the door, she heard a childish voice murmuring – 'Cold – cold – cold how long it is since I have felt a fire!' – She advanced, and saw, to her amazement, Jane Blaney, shrunk to half her usual size, and covered with rags, crouching over the embers of the fire. The housekeeper flew in terror from the spot, and roused the servants, but the vision had fled. The child was reported to have been seen several times afterwards, as diminutive in form, as though she had not grown an inch since she was ten years of age, and always crouching over a fire, whether in the turret-room or kitchen, complaining of cold and hunger, and apparently covered with rags. Her existence is still said to be protracted under these dismal circumstances, so unlike those of Lucy Gray in Wordsworth's beautiful ballad:

> Yet some will say that to this day
> She is a living child –
> That they have met sweet Lucy Gray
> Upon the lonely wild;
> O'er rough and smooth she trips along,
> And never looks behind;
> And hums a solitary song
> That whistles in the wind.

The fate of the eldest daughter was more melancholy, though less extraordinary; she was addressed by a gentleman of competent fortune and unexceptionable character: he was a Catholic, moreover; and Sir Redmond Blaney signed the marriage articles, in full satisfaction of the security of his daughter's soul, as well as of her jointure. The marriage was celebrated at the Castle of Leixlip; and, after the bride and bridegroom had retired, the guests still remained drinking to their future happiness, when suddenly, to the great alarm of Sir Redmond and his friends, loud and piercing cries were heard to issue from the part of the castle in which the bridal chamber was situated.

Some of the more courageous hurried up stairs; it was too late – the wretched bridegroom had burst, on that fatal night, into a sudden and most horrible paroxysm of insanity. The mangled form of the unfortunate and expiring lady bore attestation to the mortal virulence with which the disease had operated on the wretched husband, who died a victim to it himself after the involuntary murder of his bride. The bodies were interred, as soon as decency would permit, and the story hushed up.

Sir Redmond's hopes of Jane's recovery were diminishing every day, though he still continued to listen to every wild tale told by the domestics; and all his care was supposed to be now directed towards his only surviving daughter. Anne, living in solitude, and partaking only of the very limited education of Irish females of that period, was left very much to the servants, among whom she increased her taste for superstitious and supernatural horrors, to a degree that had a most disastrous effect on her future life.

Among the numerous menials of the Castle, there was one withered crone, who had been nurse to the late Lady Blaney's mother, and whose memory was

'Loud and piercing cries were heard to issue from the part of the castle.'

a complete *Thesaurus terrorum*. The mysterious fate of Jane first encouraged her sister to listen to the wild tales of this hag, who avouched, that at one time she saw the fugitive standing before the portrait of her late mother in one of the apartments of the Castle, and muttering to herself – 'Woe's me, woe's me! How little my mother thought her wee Jane would ever come to be what she is!' But as Anne grew older she began more 'seriously to incline' to the hag's promises that she could show her her future bridegroom, on the performance of certain ceremonies, which she at first revolted from as horrible and impious; but, finally, at the repeated instigation of the old woman, consented to act a part in. The period fixed upon for the performance of these unhallowed rites, was now approaching – it was near the 31st of October – the eventful night, when such ceremonies were, and still are supposed, in the North of Ireland, to be most potent in their effects. All day long the Crone took care to lower the mind of the young lady to the proper key of submissive and trembling credulity, by every horrible story she could relate; and she told them with frightful and supernatural energy. This woman was called *Collogue* by the family, a name equivalent to Gossip in England, or Cummer in Scotland (though her real name was Bridget Dease); and she verified the name, by the exercise of an unwearied loquacity, an indefatigable memory, and a rage for communicating, and inflicting terror, that spared no victim in the household, from the groom, whom she sent shivering to his rug, to the Lady of the Castle, over whom she felt she held unbounded sway.

The 31st of October arrived – the Castle was perfectly quiet before eleven o'clock; half an hour afterwards, the Collogue and Anne Blaney were seen gliding along a passage that led to what is called King John's Tower, where it is said that monarch received the homage of the Irish princes as Lord of Ireland and which was, at all events, the most ancient part of the structure.

The Collogue opened a small door with a key which she had secreted, about her, and urged the young lady to hurry on. Anne advanced to the postern, and stood there irresolute and trembling like a timid swimmer on the bank of an unknown stream. It was a dark autumnal evening; a heavy wind sighed among the woods of the Castle, and bowed the branches of the lower trees almost to the waves of the Liffey, which, swelled by recent rains, struggled and roared amid the stones that obstructed its channel. The steep descent from the Castle lay before her, with its dark avenue of elms; a few lights still burned in the little village of Leixlip – but from the lateness of the hour it was probable they would soon be extinguished.

The lady lingered – 'And must I go alone?' said she, foreseeing that the terrors of her fearful journey could be aggravated by her more fearful purpose.

'Ye must, or all will be spoiled,' said the hag, shading the miserable light, that did not extend its influence above six inches on the path of the victim.

'Ye must go alone – and I will watch for you here, dear, till you come back, and then see what will come to you at twelve o'clock.'

The unfortunate girl paused. 'Oh! Collogue, Collogue, if you would but come with me. Oh! Collogue, come with me, if it be but to the bottom of the castlehill.'

'If I went with you, dear, we should never reach the top of it alive again, for there are them near that would tear us both in pieces.'

'Oh! Collogue, Collogue – let me turn back then, and go to my own room – I have advanced too far, and I have done too much.'

'And that's what you have, dear, and so you must go further, and do more still, unless, when you return to your own room, you would see the likeness of *some one* instead of a handsome young bridegroom.'

The young lady looked about her for a moment, terror and wild hope trembling at her heart – then, with a sudden impulse of supernatural courage, she darted like a bird from the terrace of the Castle, the fluttering of her white garments was seen for a few moments, and then the hag who had been shading the flickering light with her hand, bolted the postern, and, placing the candle before a glazed loophole, sat down on a stone seat in the recess of the tower, to watch the event of the spell. It was an hour before the young lady returned; when her face was as pale, and her eyes as fixed, as those of a dead body, but she held in her grasp *a dripping garment,* a proof that her errand had been performed. She flung it into her companion's hands, and then stood, panting and gazing wildly about her as if she knew not where she was. The hag herself grew terrified at the insane and breathless state of her victim, and hurried her to her chamber; but here the preparations for the terrible ceremonies of the night were the first objects that struck her, and, shivering at the sight, she covered her eyes with her hands, and stood immovably fixed in the middle of the room.

It needed all the hag's persuasions (aided even by mysterious menaces), combined with the returning faculties and reviving curiosity of the poor girl, to prevail on her to go through the remaining business of the night. At length she said, as if in desperation, 'I *will* go through with it: but be in the next room; and if what I dread should happen, I will ring my father's little silver bell which I have secured for the night – and as you have a soul to be saved, Collogue, come to me at its first sound.'

The hag promised, gave her last instructions with eager and jealous minuteness, and then retired to her own room, which was adjacent to that of the young lady. Her candle had burned out, but she stirred up the embers of her turf fire, and sat, nodding over them, and smoothing the pallet from time to time, but resolved not to lie down while there was a chance of a sound from the lady's room, for which she herself, withered as her feelings were, waited with a mingled feeling of anxiety and terror.

It was now long past midnight, and all was silent as the grave throughout the Castle. The hag dozed over the embers till her head touched her knees, then started up as the sound of the bell seemed to tinkle in her ears, then dozed again, and again started as the bell appeared to tinkle more distinctly – suddenly she was roused, not by the bell, but by the most piercing and horrible cries from the neighbouring chamber. The Collogue, aghast for the first time, at the possible consequences of the mischief she might have occasioned, hastened to the room. Anne was in convulsions, and the hag was compelled reluctantly to call up the housekeeper (removing meanwhile the implements of the ceremony), and assist in applying all the specifics known at that day, burnt feathers, etc., to restore her. When they had at length succeeded, the housekeeper was dismissed, the door was bolted, and the Collogue was left alone with Anne; the subject of their conference might have been guessed at, but was not known until many years afterwards; but Anne that night held in her hand, in the shape of a weapon with the use of which neither of them was acquainted, an evidence that her chamber had been visited by a being of no earthly form.

This evidence the hag importuned her to destroy, or to remove: but she persisted with fatal tenacity in keeping it. She locked it up, however, immediately, and seemed to think she had acquired a right, since she had grappled so fearfully with the mysteries of futurity, to know all the secrets of which that weapon might yet lead to the disclosure. But from that night it was observed that her character, her manner, and even her countenance, became altered. She grew stern and solitary, shrunk at the sight of her former associates, and imperatively forbade the slightest allusion to the circumstances which had occasioned this mysterious change.

It was a few days subsequent to this event that Anne, who after dinner had left the Chaplain reading the life of St Francis Xavier to Sir Redmond, and retired to her own room to work, and, perhaps, to muse, was surprised to hear the bell at the outer gate ring loudly and repeatedly – a sound she had never heard since her first residence in the Castle; for the few guests who resorted there came, and departed as noiselessly as humble visitors at the house of a great man generally do. Straightway there rode up the avenue of elms, which we have already mentioned, a stately gentleman, followed by four servants, all mounted, the two former having pistols in their holsters, and the two latter carrying saddle-bags before them: though it was the first week in November, the dinner hour being one o'clock, Anne had light enough to notice all these circumstances. The arrival of the stranger seemed to cause much, though not unwelcome tumult in the Castle; orders were loudly and hastily given for the accommodation of the servants and horses – steps were heard traversing the numerous passages for a full hour – then all was still; and it was said that Sir Redmond had locked with his own hand the door of the room where he and the stranger sat, and desired that no one should dare to approach it. About two hours afterwards, a female servant came with orders from her master, to have a plentiful supper ready by eight o'clock, at which he desired the presence of his daughter. The family establishment was on a handsome scale for an Irish house, and Anne had only to descend to the kitchen to order the roasted chickens to be well strewed with brown sugar according to the unrefined fashion of the day, to inspect the mixing of the bowl of sago with its allowance of a bottle of port wine and a large handful of the richest spices, and to order particularly that the pease pudding should have a huge lump of cold salt butter stuck in its centre; and then, her household cares being over, to retire to her room and array herself in a robe of white damask for the occasion. At eight o'clock she was summoned to the supper-room. She came in, according to the fashion of the times, with the first dish; but as she passed through the ante-room, where the servants were holding lights and bearing the dishes, her sleeve was twitched, and the ghastly face of the Collogue pushed close to hers; while she muttered, 'Did not I say *he would come for* you, dear?' Anne's blood ran cold, but she advanced, saluted her father and the stranger with two low and distinct reverences, and then took her place at the table. Her feelings of awe and perhaps terror at the whisper of her associate, were not diminished by the appearance of the stranger; there was a singular and mute solemnity in his manner during the meal. He ate nothing. Sir Redmond appeared constrained, gloomy and thoughtful. At length, starting, he said (without naming the stranger's name), 'You will drink my daughter's health?' The stranger intimated his willingness to have that honour, but absently filled his glass with water; Anne put a few drops of wine into hers, and bowed towards him. At that moment, for the first time since they had met, she beheld his face – it was pale as that of a corpse. The deadly whiteness of his cheeks and lips, the hollow and distant sound of his voice, and the strange lustre of his large dark moveless eyes, strongly fixed on her, made her pause and even tremble as she raised the glass to her lips; she set it down, and then with another silent reverence retired to her chamber.

There she found Bridget Dease, busy in collecting the turf that burned on the hearth, for there was no grate in the apartment. 'Why are you here?' she said, impatiently.

The hag turned on her, with a ghastly grin of congratulation, 'Did not I tell you that *he* would come for you?'

'I believe he has,' said the unfortunate girl, sinking into the huge wicker chair by her bedside; 'for never did I see a mortal with such a look.'

'But is not he a fine stately gentleman?' pursued the hag.

'He looks as if he were not of this world,' said Anne.

'Of this world, or of the next,' said the hag, raising her bony fore-finger, 'mark my words – so sure as the – (here she repeated some of the horrible formularies of the 31st of October) – so sure he will be your bridegroom.'

'Then I shall be the bride of a corpse,' said Anne; 'for he I saw tonight is no living man.'

A fortnight elapsed, and whether Anne became reconciled to the features she had thought so ghastly, by the discovery that they were the handsomest she had ever beheld – and that the voice, whose sound at first was so strange and unearthly, was subdued into a tone of plaintive softness when addressing her or whether it is impossible for two young persons with unoccupied hearts to meet in the country, and meet often, to gaze silently on the same stream, wander under the same trees, and listen together to the wind that waves the branches, without experiencing an assimilation of feeling rapidly succeeding an assimilation of taste; – or whether it was from all these causes combined, but in less than a month Anne heard the declaration of the stranger's passion with many a blush, though without a sigh. He now avowed his name and rank. He stated himself to be a Scottish Baronet, of the name of Sir Richard Maxwell; family misfortunes had driven him from his country, and forever precluded the possibility of his return: he had transferred his property to Ireland, and purposed to fix his residence there for life. Such was his statement. The courtship of those days was brief and simple. Anne became the wife of Sir Richard, and, I believe, they resided with her father till his death, when they removed to their estate in the North. There they remained for several years, in tranquillity and happiness, and had a numerous family. Sir Richard's conduct was marked by but two peculiarities: he not only shunned the intercourse, but the sight of any of his countrymen, and, if he happened to hear that a Scotsman had arrived in the neighbouring town, he shut himself up till assured of the stranger's departure. The other was his custom of retiring to his own chamber and remaining invisible to his family on the anniversary of the 31st of October. The lady, who had her own associations connected with that period, only questioned him once on the subject of this seclusion, and was then solemnly and even sternly enjoined never to repeat her inquiry. Matters stood thus, somewhat mysteriously, but not unhappily, when on a sudden, without any cause assigned or assignable, Sir Richard and Lady Maxwell parted, and never more met in this world, nor was she ever permitted to see one of her children to her dying hour. He continued to live at the family mansion and she fixed her residence with a distant relative in a remote part of the country. So total was the disunion, that the name of either was never heard to pass the other's lips, from the moment of separation until that of dissolution.

Lady Maxwell survived Sir Richard forty years, living to the great age of ninety-six; and, according to a promise, previously given, disclosed to a descendent with whom she had lived, the following extraordinary circumstances.

She said that on the night of the 31st of October, about seventy-five years before, at the instigation of her ill-advising attendant, she had washed one of her garments in a place where four streams met, and performed other unhallowed ceremonies under the direction of the Collogue, in the expectation that her future husband would appear to her in her chamber at twelve o'clock that night. The critical moment arrived, but with it no lover-like form. A vision of indescribable horror approached her bed, and flinging at her an iron weapon of a shape and construction unknown to her, bade her, 'recognize her future husband *by that.*' The terrors of this visit soon deprived her of her senses; but on her recovery, she persisted, as has been said, in keeping the fearful pledge of the reality of the vision, which, on examination, appeared to be incrusted with blood. It remained concealed in the inmost drawer of her cabinet till the morning of the separation. On that morning, Sir Richard Maxwell rose before daylight to join a hunting party – he wanted a knife for some accidental purpose, and, missing his own, called to Lady Maxwell, who was still in bed, to lend him one. The lady, who was half asleep, answered, that in such a drawer of her cabinet he would find one. He went, however, to another, and the next moment she was fully awakened by seeing her husband present the terrible weapon to her throat, and threaten her with instant death unless she disclosed how she came by it. She supplicated for life, and then, in an agony of horror and contrition, told the tale of that eventful night. He gazed at her for a moment with a countenance which rage, hatred, and despair converted, as she avowed, into a living likeness of the demon-visage she had once beheld (so singularly was the fated resemblance fulfilled), and then exclaiming, 'You won me by the devil's aid, but you shall not keep me long,' left her – to meet no more in this world. Her husband's secret was not unknown to the lady, though the means by which she became possessed of it were wholly unwarrantable. Her curiosity had been strongly excited by her husband's aversion to his countrymen, and it was so – stimulated by the arrival of a Scottish gentleman in the neighbourhood some time before, who professed himself formerly acquainted with Sir Richard, and spoke mysteriously of the causes that drove him from his country – that she contrived to procure an interview with him under a feigned name, and obtained from him the knowledge of circumstances which embittered her after-life to its latest hour. His story was this:

Sir Richard Maxwell was at deadly feud with a younger brother; a family feast was proposed to reconcile them, and as the use of knives and forks was then unknown in the Highlands, the company met armed with their dirks for the purpose of carving. They drank deeply; the feast, instead of harmonizing, began to inflame their spirits; the topics of old strife were renewed; hands, that at first touched their weapons in defiance, drew them at last in fury, and in the fray, Sir Richard mortally wounded his brother. His life was with difficulty saved from the vengeance of the clan, and he was hurried towards the seacoast, near which the house stood, and concealed there till a vessel could be procured to convey him to Ireland. He embarked *on the night of the 31st of October,* and while he was traversing the deck in unutterable agony of spirit, his hand accidentally touched the dirk which he had unconsciously worn ever since the fatal night. He drew it, and, praying 'that the guilt of his brother's blood might be as far from his soul, as he could fling that weapon from his body,' sent it with all his strength into the air. This instrument he found secreted in the lady's cabinet, and whether he really believed her to have become possessed of it by supernatural means, or whether he feared his wife was a secret witness of his crime, has not been ascertained, but the result was what I have stated.

The separation took place on the discovery: – for the rest,

I know not how the truth may be,
I tell the Tale as 'twas told to me.

'Leixlip Castle', sometimes published with the title 'The Doomed Sisters', was first published in *The Literary Souvenir or, Cabinet of Poetry and Romance* in 1825.

The Haunts of the Haunter
Joseph Sheridan Le Fanu's Dublin

INTRODUCTION

Ireland has a habit of canonising its writers who forsake the Emerald Isle for the greener pastures of London, Paris and beyond. These expatriate writers transcend their Irish roots and turn away from their homeland, the land that offers them the highest praise. But Joseph Sheridan Le Fanu, unlike many Irish writers, lived his entire life in Ireland, the majority of which he spent in Dublin. And Joseph Sheridan Le Fanu, unlike George Bernard Shaw, Oscar Wilde, James Joyce, J.M. Synge and Samuel Beckett, is all but forgotten by the city in which he lived.

Joseph Thomas Sheridan Le Fanu (1814-1873) is considered by connoisseurs of the supernatural to be the grandfather of the modern ghost story.[49] A newspaper magnate by day, Le Fanu returned to the solitude of his Merrion Square home in the evening to write tales of mystery and ghostly suspense until dawn. Le Fanu is to M.R. James what Edgar Allan Poe is to Arthur Conan Doyle. M.R. James wrote of Le Fanu in his prologue to *Madame Crowl's Ghost and Other Stories of Mystery*:

> He stands absolutely in the first rank as a writer of ghost stories. That is my deliberate verdict, after reading all the supernatural tales I have been able to get hold of. Nobody sets the scene better than he, nobody touches in the effective detail more deftly.[50]

Had it not been for James's enthusiasm for the Irishman's stories, Le Fanu might have fallen into further obscurity. This tour is an attempt to breathe new life into the vanishing apparitions of Joseph Sheridan Le Fanu's years in Dublin.

DOMINICK STREET LOWER

Joseph Thomas Sheridan Le Fanu was born to Reverend Thomas Philip and Emma (*née* Dobbin) Le Fanu at 45 Dominick Street Lower, in the heart of Dublin City, on 28 August 1814. Some sources state that Le Fanu was born at the Royal Hibernian Military School in Phoenix Park, but this is incorrect, as the Le Fanu family did not move to the military school until Thomas Le Fanu was appointed chaplain there in 1815.[51]

While there is little to see on Dominick Street today, it is included as the starting point for our tour, because this was where Le Fanu's life began. Dominick Street Lower was demolished in the 1950s, and today is lined with less than picturesque Dublin Corporation housing.[52] In Le Fanu's time the north side of the city was considered more fashionable than it is today; and it was certainly more welcoming. Fortunately, a portion of northern Dominick Street is still intact. Despite looking a bit worse for wear and the presence of some unsightly exterior wiring, these Georgian houses look much as they may have in Le Fanu's day. It is this writer's opinion that you should not linger on the north side past nightfall lest harm more modern than ghostly befalls you.

Saint Mary's Church of Ease

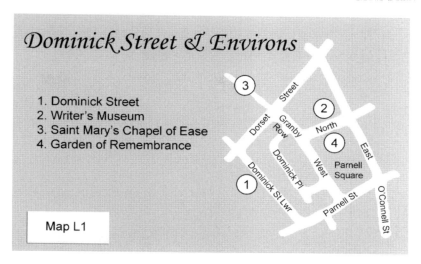

Dominick Street & Environs

1. Dominick Street
2. Writer's Museum
3. Saint Mary's Chapel of Ease
4. Garden of Remembrance

Map L1

While on the north side you will want to stop by the Dublin Writers Museum at 18 Parnell Square. The museum is a five-minute walk from Dominick Street Lower and features photographs, possessions, and artefacts of the famous Irish writers mentioned in the introduction to this book. While the museum is pleasant enough and thorough with conventional Irish fiction, there is little consideration for Ireland's fantastic and supernatural literature. Le Fanu and Bram Stoker share a small display on the first floor, while Charles Maturin and Lord Dunsany get little to no attention at all. The sole Le Fanu artefact to be found at the Writers Museum is an 1899 edition of *Uncle Silas*. (For more on the Writers Museum, see page 101.)

For the more adventurous there is Saint Mary's Chapel of Ease located *on* Saint Mary's Place – the road literally splits around it. To the locals it is known as the 'Black Church' because the stone from which it was built turns a blackish colour when it rains. The given name may be a misnomer, but the local nickname is not; there is also the local legend to consider: if one walks widdershins around the Black Church three times at midnight, one is at risk of summoning Old Scratch himself. Read Le Fanu's Faustian tale 'Sir Dominick's Bargain' (1872) and take heed.

How to Get There

Dominick Street Lower is within walking distance of O'Connell Street, the main thoroughfare in Dublin's city centre. From the north tip of O'Connell Street, take a left on Parnell Street. Dominick Street Lower is about 350 meters (400 yards) on the right.

The Dublin Writers Museum (+353 1 872 2077) is located on the north side of Parnell Square. To get to Parnell Square, continue walking north on O'Connell Street until it turns into Parnell Square East.

To get to Saint Mary's Chapel of Ease, walk north on Parnell Square West/ Granby Row and cross Dorset Street. You will find the Black Church squatting ominously in the middle of the road, waiting for you.

PHOENIX PARK & CHAPELIZOD

In 1815 Reverend Thomas Le Fanu was appointed to the chaplaincy of the Royal Hibernian Military School in Phoenix Park, where the family would live for eleven years. It was amongst the patches of forest and meadow in Phoenix Park and the quiet village of Chapelizod that young Joseph and his older brother William spent the majority of their childhood.

What was once the Royal Hibernian Military Academy is now Saint Mary's Hospital, found on the park's south side just off Chapelizod Road. Phoenix Park is billed as the largest urban park in Europe (1,752 acres)[53], and is big enough to lose oneself in for a day's exploration; the same way young Joseph and William must have on those occasionally idyllic Irish summer days. While some areas of the park are tamed into manicured sporting fields and the Royal Zoological Gardens, other parts are densely overgrown and abound with hidden secrets. It is easy to see how the wild expanse of Phoenix Park became the dark and verdant wilderness that lurked on the edges of Le Fanu's stories and novels.

Nestled between the south side of Phoenix Park and the north bank of the Liffey River is the tiny village of Chapelizod, now claimed by the ever-expanding city of Dublin as one of its many suburbs.

> The village lies in the lap of the rich and wooded valley of the Liffey and is overlooked by the high grounds of the beautiful Phoenix Park on the one side and by the ridge of the Palmerstown hills on the other. Its situation, therefore, is eminently picturesque; and factory fronts and chimneys notwithstanding, it has, I think, even in its decay, a sort of melancholy picturesqueness of its own.[54]

Chapelizod today is still separated enough from the city so as to maintain its village-like atmosphere. It has a traditional village centre, complete with a local pub and post office. Despite the march of time and an increasing number of changes, Chapelizod is similar to the way it was during Le Fanu's childhood, and still retains the 'melancholy and picturesqueness' that he described.

The Le Fanuian artefacts to be found here are the house and the churchyard made famous by Le Fanu's novel *The House by the Churchyard* (1863) and by 'Ghost Stories of Chapelizod' (1851) (see page 75).[55] Ghost story kingpin M.R. James said of *The House by the Churchyard*, 'this is a book to which I find myself returning over and over again and with no sense of disappointment.'[56] The church can be found at the end of a short alley where Chapelizod Road becomes Martin's Row. Surrounded by a wall, the church is wedged between the buildings on Martin's Row and the high wall of Phoenix Park. The gate never seems to be casually open, except on Sundays. And if it happens to be locked, there is no legal way to get in.

The main section of the church looks relatively contemporary, dating back to 1832, but modernity ends there. The church is presided over by a tall, fourteenth-century stone tower that is more akin to the remnants of a castle than

a church. This ominous tower is the first thing one sees when approaching the church. The front gates are secured with thick locks, while hideously tantalising graves crouch in the churchyard beyond, beckoning the bold:

> Bob Martin was held much in awe by truant boys who sauntered into the churchyard on Sundays to read the tomb-stones, or play leap frog over them, or climb the ivy in search of bats or sparrows' nests, or peep into the mysterious aperture under the eastern window, which opened a dim perspective of descending steps losing themselves among profounder darkness, where lidless coffins gaped horribly among tattered velvet, bones, and dust, which time and mortality had strewn there.[57]

One cannot help but imagine the young Le Fanu brothers tormenting the sexton of the day in the same manner as the boys he describes in 'Ghost Stories of Chapelizod'. Visitors to the churchyard may wish to search for the 'mysterious aperture' underneath the large round window at the rear of the church; though whether you choose to lose yourself in the mysterious aperture's profounder darkness will be left to the daring of each reader. Let it be known that neither Mr Le Fanu nor myself will be held responsible for the sightseer's safety and well-being.

The house from *The House by the Churchyard* stands on Martin's Row near the entrance to the alley leading to Saint Laurence Church. There is no discernible address on the front, though it can be easily identified as the solitary house sitting immediately in front of the church. The house's grey façade is dark and melancholy, even today, as if still haunted by Le Fanu's memorable novel. It was in this house that Mr Prosser was terrified by one of Le Fanu's notable sensationalisms:

[He] drew back at the side of the bed, and saw Mrs. Prosser lying, as for a few seconds, he mortally feared, dead, her face being motionless, white, and covered with a cold dew; and on the pillow, close beside her head, and just within the curtains, was, as he first thought, a toad – but really [a] white, fattish hand, the wrist on the pillow, and the fingers extended towards her temple.[58]

From the Chapelizod main road, find Park Lane, near the Chapelizod post office. At the end of Park Lane is a small opening in the wall to Phoenix Park. This entrance will put you on the other side of the churchyard/Phoenix Park wall, at the base of the hill where Bully Larkin in 'The Village Bully' from 'Ghost Stories of Chapelizod' encountered the phantom pugilist Long Ned:

Just as [Bully Larkin] crossed the brow of the hill which shelters the town of Chapelizod, the moon shone out for some moments with unclouded lustre and his eye, which happened to wander by the shadowy enclosures which lay at the foot of the slope, was arrested by the sight of a human figure climbing, with all the haste of one pursued, over the churchyard wall and running up the steep ascent directly towards him.[59]

While in Phoenix Park, take a moment to sit on the hill that overlooks the churchyard and village, and read 'Ghost Stories of Chapelizod' or selections from *The House by the Churchyard*. Even on a sunny day one cannot help but shiver and watch where ghostly acts played out on the stage of Le Fanu's haunted Chapelizod.

By now it is probably time for lunch. Near the Chapelizod Bridge on the main road is Mullingar House, established in 1694. The pub featured in James Joyce's

The House by the Churchyard

Finnegan's Wake (1939), and may as well serve as the setting for black Phil Slaney's pub in Le Fanu's 'The Sexton's Adventure' from 'Ghost Stories of Chapelizod'. Be wary of strangers offering free drinks – they are not always as free as they seem.

Slightly south-west of Chapelizod in Ballyfermot is a sizable park named after Le Fanu. Le Fanu Park, also known as 'The Lawns', is not much more than an average park. Those who do make the pilgrimage out there may wish to visit the site of a medieval church that once sat in the park's south-east corner.

How to Get There

'Dublin is a dreadful place,' wrote M.R. James in 1927, '…the only excursion I made was to Chapelizod to see the House by the Churchyard, which is quite unmistakable.' Monty tells us how to get there: 'The church etc. are on the right of the road as you come from Dublin, and the Phoenix Park slopes up from the wall of the churchyard, which is not very big. The river of course on the left of the road.'[60]

The Royal Hibernian Military Academy, now Saint Mary's Hospital, is located in Phoenix Park not far from the Chapelizod Gates off Chapelizod Road.

Mullingar House and the James Joyce Bistro (+353 1 620 8692) are at the intersection near the Chapelizod Bridge.

The church in *The House by the Churchyard*, known as Saint Laurence Church (+353 1 455 5639), is affiliated with the Church of Ireland. It is set just off the main road immediately behind the House. Take care not to mistake the Catholic Church of Chapelizod for Saint Laurence Church. The Catholic Church of Chapelizod is situated on Chapelizod Road east of the Chapelizod town centre. Incidentally, this Catholic church was not constructed until 1843, long after the Le Fanu family had left Dublin's haunted suburb.

TRINITY COLLEGE

In 1823, Reverend Thomas Le Fanu was appointed rector of Abington, County Limerick.[61] Three years later, the Le Fanu family moved their household to Abington, despite the growing political and religious unrest that would later be known as the Tithe War.[62] Regardless of the family's economic turmoil, Le Fanu was still able to attend university.

Returning to Dublin in the autumn of 1832, Le Fanu entered Trinity College at the age of nineteen. He studied for a career in law, but eventually his interests turned to writing and journalism. Shortly after Le Fanu enrolled at Trinity College, the *Dublin University Magazine* was first published under the editorship of his close friend Isaac Butt 1813-1879. In the years to come, Le Fanu would write for, edit, and eventually own this magazine.

Trinity College occupies a central location in Dublin, and while its high walls cut it off from the city, it continues to play a central role in Ireland's history. With its thick, twisted trees and cobblestone quadrangles, the college can be explored for hours. Bibliophiles with a nose for the antique are urged to seek out the musty, dusty and bust-lined hall of the Old Library where the *Book of Kells* is on display.

Trinity College has seen more than its fair share of supernatural fiction writers pass through its doors. It was here that notables such as Charles Maturin, 1782-1824 (*Melmoth the Wanderer*); Fitz-James O'Brien, 1828-1862 ('What Was It?'); Bram Stoker, 1847-1912 (*Dracula*); and Oscar Wilde, 1854-1900 (*The Picture of Dorian Gray*) received their educations. Unfortunately, none of their busts can be found in the Old Library. (For more on Trinity College, see pages 16 and 102.)

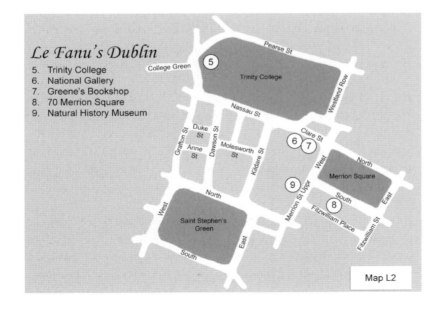

Le Fanu's Dublin

5. Trinity College
6. National Gallery
7. Greene's Bookshop
8. 70 Merrion Square
9. Natural History Museum

Map L2

Trinity College Campus

After exploring the Trinity campus, continue down Nassau Street towards Merrion Square, along the college's southern wall. Remember to thank the spirits that you are not in Captain Barton's shoes as he walked the same path home from Miss Montague's residence in 'The Watcher' (1851):

> By the side of the dead wall which bounded the College Park, the sounds followed, recommencing almost simultaneously with his own steps. The same unequal pace – sometimes slow, sometimes, for a score of yards or so, quickened to a run – was audible from behind him. Again and again he turned; quickly and stealthily he glanced over his shoulder, almost at every half-dozen steps; but no one was visible.

A short walk to the end of Nassau Street, by way of the stretch called Leinster Street, will bring you to the corner of Clare Street and Merrion Square. This corner is dominated by Dublin's National Gallery. The National Gallery is in possession of an oil painting of Le Fanu by his son George Brinsley Le Fanu. The painting is not always on display. If it is not, be sure to direct your comments to the gallery staff. If all else fails, the Jack B. Yeats exhibit is worth a gander, as are the paintings by Walter Osbourne.

Before losing yourself for the rest of the day in the National Gallery, it should be pointed out that you will be passing Dawson Street, which boasts the largest congregation of booksellers on any Dublin street. Following the premature death of Le Fanu's wife in 1858, the author largely withdrew from society, resulting in the nickname the 'Invisible Prince'. 'Popular legend had it that [Le

Fanu] could occasionally be seen at night culling the Dublin bookstalls for works on spiritualism and the supernatural.'[63] The stores on Dawson Street may not have a lot of books on spiritualism or the supernatural, but some of them do maintain rather large science fiction sections.

Greene's Bookshop

One bookshop which you will definitely want to visit is Greene's Bookshop at 16 Clare Street. The exceptionally slick website says that, 'Greene's of Clare Street has been in business since 1843', and today it does not look as if it has changed much. The walls are covered from floor to ceiling with cumbersome codices and timeworn tomes. Greene's was trading during Le Fanu's lifetime (1814-1873); could the Invisible Prince have scoured Greene's stacks by moonlight? The website does boast that, 'Many famous Irish Authors and Dublin characters were regular visitors to our shop in days gone by.' Perhaps Greene's used to have later opening hours as well.

How to Get There

Trinity College is one of Dublin's central landmarks. Its main entrance is at the junction of College Green, College Street and Grafton Street, a five-minute jaunt from O'Connell Bridge.[64] The *Book of Kells* is on display in the Old Library (+353 1 677 2941) and is highly recommended.

The top of Dawson Street, with its myriad booksellers, is across the street from Trinity College's Arts Building/Nassau Street entrance.

The National Gallery (+353 1 661 5133) and Greene's Bookshop (+353 1 676 2554) are virtually neighbours on Clare Street, an extension of Nassau Street following the south wall of Trinity College west towards Merrion Square. Both are a fifteen-minute stroll from the front gates of Trinity College.

70 Merrion Square

Le Fanu moved with his wife Susanna (*née* Bennett) to 70 Merrion Square (then number 18), a prestigious address in one of Dublin's many Georgian neighbourhoods. The house originally belonged to the Bennett family and became the Le Fanu home in the early 1850s. It was in this house that Joseph Sheridan Le Fanu wrote the majority of his literary output. Le Fanu's son George Brinsley describes the author's peculiar habits:

> He wrote mostly in bed at night, using copy-books for his manuscript. He always had two candles by his side on a small table; one of these dimly glimmering tapers would be left burning while he took a brief sleep. Then, when he awoke about 2 a.m. amid the darkling shadows of the heavy furnishings and hangings of his old-fashioned room, he would brew himself some strong tea – which he drank copiously and frequently throughout the day – and write for a couple of hours in that eerie period of the night when human vitality is at its lowest ebb.[65]

Up until the early 1860s, Le Fanu's publishing history consisted of two novels and a book of short stories. It was not until his wife's death in 1858, followed by his mother's death in 1861, that he commenced writing seriously and prolifically.

Merrion Square is the most celebrated and well-known of Dublin's Georgian squares. Number 70 is on the square's south side and is no longer residential. A brass plaque that says 'Arts Council' is displayed near the front door. A small, circular plaque between the windows reads simply:

70 Merrion Square

Over the years the square has been home to other people associated with the mystical, spectral and Swedenborgian. Number 82 is the former home of statesman and poet William Butler Yeats (1865-1939), while 84 Merrion Square South is the former workplace of George William Russell (Æ) (1867-1935). The Wilde family lived on the north side of the square at number 1. This was the childhood home of Oscar Wilde.[66] In fact, 'the Wilde children occasionally played at No. [70].'[67] Le Fanu's neighbourhood has always kept good company.

For those with an interest in dead animals, Ireland's Natural History Museum, known locally as the 'Dead Zoo' is just south of the National Gallery on Merrion Square West. The building is little more than an enormous mausoleum housing a massive Victorian-style collection of well-preserved animals from Ireland and beyond. There is little information about each of the displays, but they are captivating nevertheless. The museum has literally thousands of specimens. The petrified skeleton of a prehistoric giant Irish elk, a South American pygmy squirrel, a thylacine (Australia's extinct marsupial wolf) and everything in between can be found within the museum's walls. The bones of an enormous blue whale suspended overhead are alone enough to impress.

How to Get There

Both Merrion Square and the Natural History Museum (+353 1 677 7444) are a fifteen-minute walk from Trinity College or a twenty-five minute walk from O'Connell Bridge.

AUNGIER STREET & ENVIRONS

'An Account of Some Strange Disturbances in Aungier Street' (1853) is one of Le Fanu's most memorable Dublin ghost stories. The tale tells of two cousins who take up residence in a haunted house on Dublin's Aungier Street. Aungier Street and the entire length of road from Dame Street to the Grand Canal contain houses of considerable antiquity, some of which must at least furnish an authentic ghost or two.

With your back to Trinity College, Great George's Street South is the first street left off Dame Street. The street is a mixture of sleekly restored shop fronts as well as some of the most crumbling and decayed buildings in central Dublin. A walk down Great George's Street South will give you a sense of Dublin spanning the past 200 years.

About a block after the George's Street Arcade, distinctive for its red turrets, Great George's Street South becomes Aungier Street. While Aungier Street is not as striking as Great George's Street South, a few ancient buildings still stick up like neglected teeth. It was Aungier Street where, '...Uncle Ludlow – Tom's father – while we were attending lectures, purchased three or four old houses.' 'An Account of Some Strange Disturbances in Aungier Street' is the story of a house with a bad history. The narrator Richard and his cousin Tom are haunted by all manner of ghostly noises and apparitions until the ghastly climax:

> I jumped out of bed, clutched the poker as I passed the expiring fire, and in a moment was upon the lobby. The sound had ceased by this time – the dark and chill were discouraging; and, guess my horror, when I saw, or thought I saw, a black monster, whether in the shape of a man or a bear I could not say, standing with its back to the wall, on the lobby, facing me, with a pair of great greenish eyes shining dimly out.[68]

While Richard stood steadfast in the face of what may or may not have been a sinister bear, the ghostly occurrences were much too unnerving for Cousin Tom:

> 'Now, Dick, you will hardly believe me, when I assure you, that for many nights after this last experience, I did not go to my room at all. I used to sit up for a while in the drawing-room after you had gone up to your bed, and then steal down softly to the hall-door, let myself out, and sit in the "Robin Hood" tavern until the last guest went off; and then I got through the night like a sentry, pacing the streets till morning.'[69]

It is anyone's guess which building, if any, was intended to be Le Fanu's spectre-infested house, but the inspiration for the Robin Hood tavern may still be extant. On the corner of Aungier Street and York Street is a prominent local pub known as The Swan Bar. The Swan Bar has been serving pints since 1897, though the premises have been a public house since 1739.[70] This is well before Le Fanu's time and probably before the story's setting. Could this be where the terrified

Saint Kevin's Park

Tom spent his sleepless nights? Today this long-established local is an inviting place to take a break, rendering sinister bears and other excuses completely unnecessary if one wants to stop in for a quick pint.

Also on Aungier Street you will find number 12, home to the pub known as J.J. Smyth's, and the birthplace of the balladeer and poet Thomas Moore (1779-1852). Moore is best known for 'The Last Rose of Summer' from his *Irish Melodies,* published as ten volumes between 1808 and 1832. Today, the melodies of mighty good jazz and blues can be heard emanating from J.J. Smyth's on nearly any given night.

If you continue heading south on Aungier Street, you will find the tiny Digges Street where Richard and Tom took temporary lodgings from the haunted house. Much like Dominick Street Lower, there is little to see here, as Digges Street is now a knot of Dublin Corporation housing that replaced the Georgian buildings decades ago.

Continue south on Aungier Street. Once you pass Cuffe Street, Aungier Street turns into Wexford Street for one block before giving way to Camden Street Lower. Where Wexford Street meets Camden Street Lower you will find a small and barely noticeable side street known as Camden Row. A short way down Camden Row you will find one of Dublin's best-kept secrets: Saint Kevin's Park.

Saint Kevin's Park, a mere one hundred metres from the noise of urban Dublin, is as secluded and as quiet as a grave. In fact, up until the 1960s, Saint Kevin's Park *was* a graveyard. The roofless, one-roomed church, the remains of which are still in the park, was built in the late eighteenth century.[71] Those buried in Saint Kevin's churchyard, the remains of whom are *not* still in the park, have been re-interred elsewhere.[72] The headstones, however, remain; chipped, broken, and weathered, they lean decoratively against the side of the church and the interior of the park's wall. Although Saint Kevin's function changed from churchyard to park in the 1960s,

The Bleeding Horse

it retains its peaceful atmosphere, and is worth a stopover for that alone. A small memorial to the family of the poet Thomas Moore can also be found in the park.

If you do not care for the peaceful solitude of Saint Kevin's, you may wish to proceed directly to the more boisterous Bleeding Horse pub at the intersection of Camden Street and Charlotte Way. A pub has stood on this site since the 1640s, and though it has been rebuilt, remodelled and renamed in the intervening years, the pub still manages to maintain a historic atmosphere.[73] The original Bleeding Horse is given a mention in Le Fanu's first novel *The Cock and the Anchor* (1845).

If you decide to relax for a while in this quaintly modern pub, make your way to the second floor and have a pint or two in the presence of Joseph himself. On the wall of a comfortable nook you will find a small, framed portrait of J.S. Le Fanu next to the page from *The Cock and the Anchor* on which he mentions the Bleeding Horse.

When you leave the Bleeding Horse, be sure to exit from the side door. You will find just outside the doorway an engraved flagstone that gets trampled nightly by the Bleeding Horse's oblivious and obliviated patrons. It reads thusly:

The engraved footstone at the Bleeding Horse's front entrance is reserved, not surprisingly, for a quote from James Joyce's *Ulysses* (1922). I personally never use that entrance.

How to Get There

The Swan Bar (+353 1 475 2722) is located at the corner of Aungier Street and York Street. J.J. Smyth's (+353 1 475 2565) is at the corner of Aungier Street and Aungier Place, while the Bleeding Horse (+353 1 475 2705) is just a bit further south at the intersection of Camden Street and Charlotte Way.

The locations in section five are, more or less, in a straight line on the same street, or more accurately, series of streets. Starting from Dame Street, it is easiest to begin by walking south on Great George's Street South.

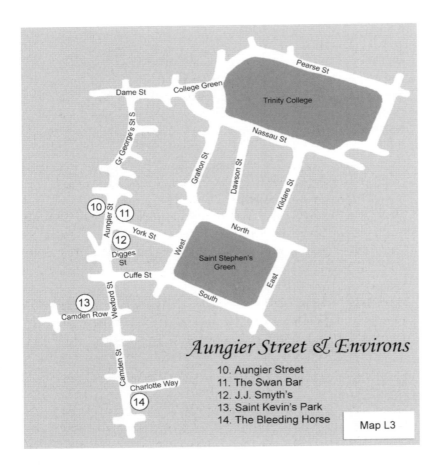

Aungier Street & Environs

10. Aungier Street
11. The Swan Bar
12. J.J. Smyth's
13. Saint Kevin's Park
14. The Bleeding Horse

Map L3

MOUNT JEROME CEMETERY

In the years following the deaths of his wife and his mother, Le Fanu became increasingly withdrawn into his Merrion Square home. Along with his self-imposed social exile came a profound increase in his literary output. From his mother's death in 1861 to his own death in 1873, Le Fanu had fourteen books published and more than doubled his body of short stories. Considering that from 1845 until 1862 he had only three books published, this is an astonishing feat. In the last decade of his life Le Fanu's writing was admired by such notables as Charles Dickens, Wilkie Collins and, almost undoubtedly, Charlotte Brontë.[74] But in the years following his death, Le Fanu's popularity would not last.

On 7 February 1873, Joseph Sheridan Le Fanu passed away in his sleep.[75] While one biographer claims that Le Fanu died of a heart attack[76], another makes no real assertion and leaves the explanation up to Le Fanu's daughter Emma:

> He had almost got over a bad attack of Bronchitis but his strength gave way & he sank very quickly & died in his sleep....His face looks so happy with a beautiful smile on it. We were quite unprepared for the end. My brother Philip & I never left him during his illness & we were so hopeful and happy about him even the day before he seemed to be so much better.[77]

Le Fanu was interred at Mount Jerome Cemetery in Harold's Cross on 11 February 1873. He was laid to rest in the Bennett Family tomb, 'beside his wife and five other members of the Bennett Family.'[78]

Mount Jerome, a labyrinthine, 47-acre Victorian cemetery dating back to 1836, is a most appropriate resting place for a writer of ghost stories and historical novels. Imagine grandiose Victorian tombs subjected to one hundred years of decay and you have just conjured up a picture of Mount Jerome Cemetery.

Weathered monuments clutter every square inch of the grounds and not a single blade of grass is to be found amongst the rubble of toppled monuments and caved-in capstones. Rough paths weave around the stones like sepulchral worms. To the astute explorer, bits of bone, too large to be the bones of small animals killed by foxes, can sometimes be found littering the ground. This is the Père-Lachaise of Dublin, complete with its own member of the Wilde family.[79]

Despite being eroded so badly that few words can be discerned, the Bennett/Le Fanu vault is easy to locate. Follow the main road (the Avenue) from the front gates on Harold's Cross Road towards the chapel. Take the first right on to the Low Walk. Follow the Low Walk until it intersects with the Long Walk and the Nun's Walk, which continues along the cemetery wall. Continue on the Nun's Walk until it diverges from the wall, dipping in towards the cemetery. The Bennett/Le Fanu vault is located at the interior tip of this divergence.[80] The flat, Keane

The Long Walk,
Mount Jerome Cemetery

The Bennett/Le Fanu Vault

limestone slab is dark grey, and barely retains the names of those entombed therein. Halfway down the slab, close scrutiny will reveal the faded engraving:

JOSEPH SHERIDAN LE FANU 1873

Mount Jerome Cemetery is a private cemetery, meaning each plot is owned by the family (or benefactor) of the occupants. Because each plot is essentially a private piece of land, and because the cemetery is not owned by the city, maintenance and upkeep is mainly the responsibility of the family. Many of the plots and stones are so old that there are no remaining relatives; consequently a large portion of the cemetery, including the Bennett/Le Fanu vault, has fallen into ruin.

Those wishing to make the worthwhile trek to Mount Jerome Cemetery should be warned that the front gates close promptly at four o'clock. Those unfortunate

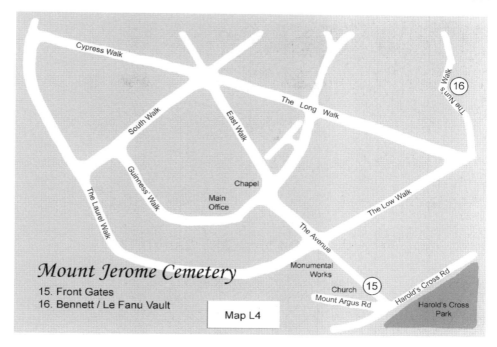

Mount Jerome Cemetery

15. Front Gates
16. Bennett / Le Fanu Vault

Map L4

enough to be caught within the cemetery walls after closing will be comforted to know that, other than acquiring stark white hair and becoming quite listless by morning, survivors of a night in Mount Jerome are usually quite healthy.

How to Get There

Mount Jerome Cemetery in Harold's Cross can be reached by taking a bus from the city centre. It can also be reached on foot, but is a good thirty minutes from Saint Patrick's Cathedral, from which the cemetery lies directly south.

OTHER PLACES OF INTEREST

Le Fanu lived in many more houses in Dublin and the surrounding area, though they are too numerous or inconsequential to list. However, for completists and obsessives, here are a few more.

Le Fanu lived in number 2 Nelson Street on the north side of the city during his days at law school. Not far from Nelson Street was 3 Gloucester Place. It was at this address that Le Fanu's wayward son Thomas Philip (1847-1879), who became further estranged from the family after his father's death, passed away not long after his father.

From here it is perhaps best to quote Le Fanu's biographer W.J. McCormack:

During the ten years of their marriage, the Le Fanus had spent various prolonged periods at Bray, Malahide, and Kingstown....It is difficult to follow their movements during this period. They lived in Warrington Place till 1850, and sometime shortly afterwards moved into Merrion Square with the Bennetts. [81]

Warrington Place is where Mount Street Lower meets the Grand Canal. To get there, walk east along Merrion Square North, which turns into Mount Street Lower before it meets the Grand Canal. Warrington Place is a strip of small cottages along the northern side of the canal.

Malahide and Bray, the north tip and south tip of Dublin, respectively, are both nice places to visit for reasons other than Le Fanu. Malahide boasts an early twelfth-century haunted castle, while Bray has a nice coastal beach dominated at one end by a small mountain, Bray Head. Le Fanu lived at 11 Brennan's Terrace, Bray for a few months in 1864 recovering from influenza and bronchitis.

What was formerly known as Kingstown is now the town (and Dublin suburb) of Dún Laoghaire on the Irish Sea. Malahide, Dún Laoghaire and Bray are all stops on the Dublin Area Rapid Transit (DART) line. Dún Laoghaire and Bray are on the southern line, while Malahide is on the northern line.

For those of you who cannot get enough of ghosts and ghouls of the night, there is always the most excellent Dublin Ghost Bus tour. The bus will take you through the streets of Dublin at night, while the guide weaves tales of Dublin's haunted history. The tour guides/storytellers are impressive, combining campy thrills and genuine chills. And the tour is not confined to the bus; there are a few stops where passengers are allowed to disembark and wander around some of the more shadowy parts of the city. The tour is entertaining and highly recommended. The Dublin Ghost Bus leaves nightly from Dublin Bus' headquarters at 59 Upper O'Connell Street. The phone number for booking and more information is +353 1 873 4222.

EPILOGUE

Today, only small and crumbling memorials across the city pay silent tribute to Joseph Sheridan Le Fanu's place in Dublin's literary history. From the virtually non-existent display at the Writers Museum, to the trampled and alcohol-soaked engraving outside the Bleeding Horse, to the weathered capstone of the Bennett/Le Fanu family vault, the memory of Joseph Le Fanu is receding into the solitude of the past – in much the same way Le Fanu himself did in the later years of his life.

But for those who inspect the corners of Dublin's forgotten places closely enough, memories of the haunted haunter will always be found. And while laurels of praise are showered upon Joyce, Beckett and Shaw, Joseph Thomas Sheridan Le Fanu, author of fourteen novels and some of the world's most memorable and influential ghost stories, may forever remain Dublin's Invisible Prince.

Ghost Stories of Chapelizod

by Joseph Sheridan Le Fanu

Take my word for it, there is no such thing as an ancient village, especially if it has seen better days, un-illustrated by its legends of terror. You might as well expect to find a decayed cheese without mites, or an old house without rats, as an antique and dilapidated town without an authentic population of goblins. Now, although this class of inhabitants are in nowise amenable to the police authorities, yet, as their demeanour directly affects the comforts of her Majesty's subjects, I cannot but regard it as a grave omission that the public have hitherto been left without any statistical returns of their numbers, activity, etc., etc. And I am persuaded that a Commission to inquire into and report upon the numerical strength, habits, haunts, etc., etc. of supernatural agents resident in Ireland, would be a great deal more innocent and entertaining than half the Commissions for which the country pays, and at least as instructive. This I say, more from a sense of duty, and to deliver my mind of a grave truth, than with any hope of seeing the suggestion adopted. But, I am sure, my readers will deplore with me that the comprehensive powers of belief, and apparently illimitable leisure, possessed by parliamentary commissions of inquiry, should never have been applied to the subject I have named, and that the collection of that species of information should be confided to the gratuitous and desultory labours of individuals, who, like myself, have other occupations to attend to. This, however, by the way.

Among the village outposts of Dublin, Chapelizod once held a considerable, if not a foremost rank. Without mentioning its connexion with the history of the great Kilmainham Preceptory of the Knights of St John, it will be enough to remind the reader of its ancient and celebrated Castle, not one vestige of which now remains, and of the fact that it was for, we believe, some centuries, the summer residence of the Viceroys of Ireland, The circumstance of its being up, we believe, to the period at which that corps was disbanded, the head-quarters of the Royal Irish Artillery, gave it also a consequence of a humbler, but not less substantial kind. With these advantages in its favour, it is not wonderful that the town exhibited at one time an air of substantial and semi-aristocratic prosperity unknown to Irish villages in modern times.

A broad street, with a well-paved foot-path, and houses as lofty as were at that time to be found in the fashionable streets of Dublin; a goodly stone-fronted barrack; an ancient church, vaulted beneath, and with a tower clothed from its summit to its base with the richest ivy; an humble Roman Catholic chapel; a steep bridge spanning the Liffey, and a great old mill at the near end of it, were the principal features of the town. These, or at least most of them, remain still, but the greater part in a very changed and forlorn condition. Some of them indeed are superseded, though not obliterated by modern erections, such as the bridge, the chapel, and the church in part; the rest forsaken by the order who originally raised them, and delivered up to poverty, and in some cases to absolute decay.

The village lies in the lap of the rich and wooded valley of the Liffey, and is overlooked by the high grounds of the beautiful Phoenix Park on the one side, and by the ridge of the Palmerstown hills on the other. Its situation, therefore, is eminently picturesque; and factory-fronts and chimneys notwithstanding, it has, I think, even in its decay, a sort of melancholy picturesqueness of its own. Be that as it may, I mean to relate two or three stories of that sort which may be read with very good effect by a blazing fire on a shrewd winter's night, and are all directly connected with the altered and somewhat melancholy little town I have named. The first I shall relate concerns…

THE VILLAGE BULLY

About thirty years ago there lived in the town of Chapelizod an ill-conditioned fellow of Herculean strength, well known throughout the neighbourhood by the title of Bully Larkin. In addition to his remarkable physical superiority, this fellow had acquired a degree of skill as a pugilist which alone would have made him formidable. As it was, he was the autocrat of the village, and carried not the sceptre in vain. Conscious of his superiority, and perfectly secure of impunity, he lorded it over his fellows in a spirit of cowardly and brutal insolence, which made him hated even more profoundly than he was feared.

Upon more than one occasion he had deliberately forced quarrels upon men whom he had singled out for the exhibition of his savage prowess; and in every encounter his over-matched antagonist had received an amount of 'punishment' which edified and appalled the spectators, and in some instances left ineffaceable scars and lasting injuries after it.

Bully Larkin's pluck had never been fairly tried. For, owing to his prodigious superiority in weight, strength, and skill, his victories had always been certain and easy; and in proportion to the facility with which he uniformly smashed an antagonist, his pugnacity and insolence were inflamed. He thus became an odious nuisance in the neighbourhood, and the terror of every mother who had a son, and of every wife who had a husband who possessed a spirit to resent insult, or the smallest confidence in his own pugilistic capabilities.

Now it happened that there was a young fellow named Ned Moran – better known by the soubriquet of 'Long Ned', from his slender, lathy proportions – at that time living in the town. He was, in truth, a mere lad, nineteen years of age, and fully twelve years younger than the stalwart bully. This, however, as the reader will see, secured for him no exemption from the dastardly provocations of the ill-conditioned pugilist. Long Ned, in an evil hour, had thrown eyes of affection upon a certain buxom damsel, who, notwithstanding Bully Larkin's amorous rivalry, inclined to reciprocate them.

I need not say how easily the spark of jealousy, once kindled, is blown into a flame, and how naturally, in a coarse and ungoverned nature, it explodes in acts of violence and outrage.

'The bully' watched his opportunity, and contrived to provoke Ned Moran, while drinking in a public-house with a party of friends, into an altercation, in the course of which he failed not to put such insults upon his rival as manhood could not tolerate. Long Ned, though a simple, good-natured sort of fellow, was by no means deficient in spirit, and retorted in a tone of defiance which edified the more timid, and gave his opponent the opportunity he secretly coveted.

Bully Larkin challenged the heroic youth, whose pretty face he had privately consigned to the mangling and bloody discipline he was himself so capable of administering. The quarrel, which he had himself contrived to get up, to a certain degree covered the ill blood and malignant premeditation which inspired his proceedings, and Long Ned, being full of generous ire and whiskey punch, accepted the gauge of battle on the instant. The whole party, accompanied by a mob of idle men and boys, and in short by all who could snatch a moment from the calls of business, proceeded in slow procession through the old gate into the Phoenix Park, and mounting the hill over-looking the town, selected near its summit a level spot on which to decide the quarrel.

The combatants stripped, and a child might have seen in the contrast presented by the slight, lank form and limbs of the lad, and the muscular and massive build of his veteran antagonist, how desperate was the chance of poor Ned Moran.

'Seconds' and 'bottle-holders' – selected of course for their love of the game – were appointed, and 'the fight' commenced.

I will not shock my readers with a description of the cool-blooded butchery that followed. The result of the combat was what anybody might have predicted. At the eleventh round, poor Ned refused to 'give in'; the brawny pugilist, unhurt, in good wind, and pale with concentrated and as yet unslaked revenge, had the gratification of seeing his opponent seated upon his second's knee, unable to hold up his head, his left arm disabled; his face a bloody, swollen, and shapeless mass; his breast scarred and bloody, and his whole body panting and quivering with rage and exhaustion.

'Give in, Ned, my boy,' cried more than one of the bystanders.

'Never, never,' shrieked he, with a voice hoarse and choking.

Time being 'up', his second placed him on his feet again. Blinded with his own blood, panting and staggering, he presented but a helpless mark for the blows of his stalwart opponent. It was plain that a touch would have been sufficient to throw him to the earth. But Larkin had no notion of letting him off so easily. He closed with him without striking a blow (the effect of which, prematurely dealt, would have been to bring him at once to the ground, and so put an end to the combat), and getting his battered and almost senseless head under his arm, fast in that peculiar 'fix' known to the fancy pleasantly by the name of 'chancery', he held him firmly, while with monotonous and brutal strokes he beat his fist, as it seemed, almost into his face. A cry of 'shame' broke from the crowd, for it was plain that the beaten man was now insensible, and supported only by the Herculean arm of the bully. The round and the fight ended by his hurling him upon the ground, falling upon him at the same time with his knee upon his chest.

The bully rose, wiping the perspiration from his white face with his blood-stained hands, but Ned lay stretched and motionless upon the grass. It was impossible to get him upon his legs for another round. So he was carried down, just as he was, to the pond which then lay close to the old Park gate, and his head and body were washed beside it. Contrary to the belief of all he was not dead. He was carried home, and after some months to a certain extent recovered. But he never held up his head again, and before the year was over he had died of consumption. Nobody could doubt how the disease had been induced, but there was no actual proof to connect the cause and effect, and the ruffian Larkin escaped the vengeance of the law. A strange retribution, however, awaited him.

After the death of Long Ned, he became less quarrelsome than before, but more sullen and reserved. Some said 'he took it to heart', and others, that his conscience was not at ease about it. Be this as it may, however, his health did not suffer by reason of his presumed agitations, nor was his worldly prosperity marred by the blasting curses with which poor Moran's enraged mother pursued him; on the contrary, he had rather risen in the world, and obtained regular and well-remunerated employment from the Chief Secretary's gardener, at the other side of the Park. He still lived in Chapelizod, whither, on the close of his day's work, he used to return across the Fifteen Acres.

It was about three years after the catastrophe we have mentioned, and late in the autumn, when, one night, contrary to his habit, he did not appear at the house where he lodged, neither had he been seen anywhere, during the evening, in the village. His hours of return had been so very regular, that his absence excited considerable surprise, though, of course, no actual alarm; and, at the usual hour, the house was closed for the night, and the absent lodger consigned to the mercy of the elements, and the care of his presiding star. Early in the morning, however, he was found lying in a state of utter helplessness upon the slope immediately overlooking the Chapelizod gate. He had been smitten with a paralytic stroke: his right side was dead; and it was many weeks before he had recovered his speech sufficiently to make himself at all understood.

He then made the following relation: He had been detained, it appeared, later than usual, and darkness had closed before he commenced his homeward walk across the Park. It was a moonlit night, but masses of ragged clouds were slowly drifting across the heavens. He had not encountered a human figure, and no sounds but the softened rush of the wind sweeping through bushes and hollows met his ear.

These wild and monotonous sounds, and the utter solitude which surrounded him, did not, however, excite any of those uneasy sensations which are ascribed to superstition, although he said he did feel depressed, or, in his own phraseology, 'lonesome'. Just as he crossed the brow of the hill which shelters the town of Chapelizod, the moon shone out for some moments with unclouded lustre, and his eye, which happened to wander by the shadowy enclosures which lay at the foot of the slope, was arrested by the sight of a human figure climbing, with all the haste of one pursued, over the church-yard wall, and running up the steep ascent directly towards him. Stories of 'Resurrectionists' crossed his recollection, as he observed this suspicious-looking figure. But he began, momentarily, to be aware with a sort of fearful instinct which he could not explain, that the running figure was directing his steps, with a sinister purpose, towards himself.

The form was that of a man with a loose coat about him, which, as he ran, he disengaged, and as well as Larkin could see, for the moon was again wading in clouds, threw from him. The figure thus advanced until within some two score yards of him, it arrested its speed, and approached with a loose, swaggering gait. The moon again shone out bright and clear, and, gracious God! What was the spectacle before him? He saw as distinctly as if he had been presented there in the flesh, Ned Moran, himself, stripped naked from the waist upward, as if for pugilistic combat, and drawing towards him in silence. Larkin would have shouted, prayed, cursed, fled across the Park, but he was absolutely powerless; the apparition stopped within a few steps, and leered on him with a ghastly mimicry of the defiant stare with which pugilists strive to cow one another before combat. For a time, which he could not so much as conjecture, he was held in the fascination of that unearthly gaze, and at last the thing, whatever it was, on a sudden swaggered close up to him with extended palms. With an

'The running figure was directing his steps, with a sinister purpose, towards himself.'

impulse of horror, Larkin put out his hand to keep the figure off, and their palms touched – at least, so he believed – for a thrill of unspeakable agony, running through his arm, pervaded his entire frame, and he fell senseless to the earth.

Though Larkin lived for many years after, his punishment was terrible. He was incurably maimed; and being unable to work, he was forced, for existence, to beg alms of those who had once feared and flattered him. He suffered, too, increasingly, under his own horrible interpretation of the preternatural encounter which was the beginning of all his miseries. It was vain to endeavour to shake his faith in the reality of the apparition, and equally vain, as some compassionately did, to try to persuade him that the greeting with which his vision closed was intended, while inflicting a temporary trial, to signify a compensating reconciliation.

'No, no,' he used to say, 'all won't do. I know the meaning of it well enough; it is a challenge to meet him in the other world – in Hell, where I am going – that's what it means, and nothing else.'

And so, miserable and refusing comfort, he lived on for some years, and then died, and was buried in the same narrow churchyard which contains the remains of his victim.

I need hardly say, how absolute was the faith of the honest inhabitants, at the time when I heard the story, in the reality of the preternatural summons which, through the portals of terror, sickness, and misery, had summoned Bully Larkin to his long, last home, and that, too, upon the very ground on which he had signalised the guiltiest triumph of his violent and vindictive career.

I recollect another story of the preternatural sort, which made no small sensation, some five-and-thirty years ago, among the good gossips of the town; and, with your leave, courteous reader, I shall relate it.

THE SEXTON'S ADVENTURE

Those who remember Chapelizod a quarter of a century ago, or more, may possibly recollect the parish sexton. Bob Martin was held much in awe by truant boys who sauntered into the churchyard on Sundays, to read the tomb-stones, or play leap frog over them, or climb the ivy in search of bats of sparrows' nests, or peep into the mysterious aperture under the eastern window, which opened a dim perspective of descending steps losing themselves among profounder darkness, where lidless coffins gaped horribly among tattered velvet, bones, and dust, which time and mortality had strewn there. Of such horribly curious and otherwise enterprising juveniles, Bob was, of course, the special scourge and terror. But terrible as was the official aspect of the sexton, and repugnant as his lank form, clothed in rusty, sable vesture, his small, frosty visage, suspicious grey eyes, and rusty, brown scratch-wig, might appear to all notions of genial frailty; it was yet true, that Bob Martin's severe morality sometimes nodded, and that Bacchus did not always solicit him in vain.

Bob had a curious mind, a memory well stored with 'merry tales', and tales of terror. His profession familiarized him with graves and goblins, and his tastes with weddings, wassail, and sly frolics of all sorts. And as his personal recollections ran back nearly three score years into the perspective of the village history, his fund of local anecdote was copious, accurate, and edifying.

As his ecclesiastical revenues were by no means considerable, he was not unfrequently obliged, for the indulgence of his tastes, to arts which were, at the best, undignified.

He frequently invited himself when his entertainers had forgotten to do so; he dropped in accidentally upon small drinking parties of his acquaintance in public houses, and entertained them with stories, queer or terrible, from his inexhaustible reservoir, never scrupling to accept an acknowledgment in the shape of a hot whiskey-punch, or whatever else was going.

There was at that time a certain atrabilious publican, called Philip Slaney, established in a shop nearly opposite the old turnpike. This man was not, when left to himself, immoderately given to drinking; but being naturally of a saturnine complexion, and his spirits constantly requiring a fillip, he acquired a prodigious liking for Bob Martin's company. The sexton's society, in fact, gradually became the solace of his existence, and he seemed to lose his constitutional melancholy in the fascination of his sly jokes and marvellous stories.

This intimacy did not redound to the prosperity or reputation of the convivial allies. Bob Martin drank a good deal more punch than was good for his health, or consistent with the character of an ecclesiastical functionary. Philip Slaney, too, was drawn into similar indulgences, for it was hard to resist the genial seductions of his gifted companion; and as he was obliged to pay for both, his purse was believed to have suffered even more than his head and liver.

Be this as it may, Bob Martin had the credit of having made a drunkard of 'black Phil Slaney' – for by this cognomen was he distinguished; and Phil Slaney had also the reputation of having made the sexton, if possible, a 'bigger bliggard' than ever. Under these circumstances, the accounts of the concern opposite the turnpike became somewhat entangled; and it came to pass one drowsy summer morning, the weather being at once sultry and cloudy, that Phil Slaney went into a small back parlour, where he kept his books, and which commanded, through its dirty window-panes, a full view of a dead wall, and having bolted the door, he took a loaded pistol, and clapping the muzzle in his mouth, blew the upper part of his skull through the ceiling.

This horrid catastrophe shocked Bob Martin extremely; and partly on this account, and partly because having been, on several late occasions, found at night in a state of abstraction, bordering on insensibility, upon the high road, he had been threatened with dismissal; and, as some said, partly also because of the difficulty of finding anybody to 'treat' him as poor Phil Slaney used to do, he for a time forswore alcohol in all its combinations, and became an eminent example of temperance and sobriety.

Bob observed his good resolutions, greatly to the comfort of his wife, and the edification of the neighbourhood, with tolerable punctuality. He was seldom tipsy, and never drunk, and was greeted by the better part of society with all the honours of the prodigal son.

Now it happened, about a year after the grisly event we have mentioned, that the curate having received, by the post, due notice of a funeral to be consummated in the churchyard of Chapelizod, with certain instructions respecting the site of the grave, despatched a summons for Bob Martin, with a view to communicate to that functionary these official details.

It was a lowering autumn night: piles of lurid thunder-clouds, slowly rising from the earth, had loaded the sky with a solemn and boding canopy of storm. The growl of distant thunder was heard afar off upon the dull, still air, and all nature seemed, as it were, hushed and cowering under the oppressive influence of the approaching tempest.

It was past nine o'clock when Bob, putting on his official coat of seedy black, prepared to attend his professional superior.

'Bobby, darlin',' said his wife, before she delivered the hat she held in her hand to his keeping, 'sure you won't, Bobby, darlin' – you won't – you know what.'

'I don't know what,' he retorted, smartly, grasping at his hat.

'You won't be throwing up the little finger, Bobby, acushla?' she said, evading his grasp.

'Arrah, why would I, woman? There, give me my hat, will you?'

'But won't you promise me, Bobby darlin' – won't you alanna?'

'Ay, ay, to be sure I will – why not? – There, give me my hat, and let me go.'

'Ay, but you're not promisin', Bobby, mavourneen; you're not promisin' all the time.'

'Well, divil carry me if I drink a drop till I come back again,' said the sexton, angrily; 'Will that do you? And now will you give me my hat?'

'Here it is, darlin',' she said, 'and God send you safe back.'

And with this parting blessing she closed the door upon his retreating figure, for it was now quite dark, and resumed her knitting till his return, very much relieved; for she thought he had of late been oftener tipsy than was consistent with his thorough reformation, and feared the allurements of the half dozen 'publics' which he had at that time to pass on his way to the other end of the town.

They were still open, and exhaled a delicious reek of whiskey, as Bob glided wistfully by them; but he stuck his hands in his pockets and looked the other way, whistling resolutely, and filling his mind with the image of the curate and anticipations of his coming fee. Thus he steered his morality safely through these rocks of offence, and reached the curate's lodging in safety.

He had, however, an unexpected sick call to attend, and was not at home, so that Bob Martin had to sit in the hall and amuse himself with the devil's tattoo until his return. This, unfortunately, was very long delayed, and it must have been fully twelve o'clock when Bob Martin set out upon his homeward way. By this time the storm had gathered to a pitchy darkness, the bellowing thunder was heard among the rocks and hollows of the Dublin mountains, and the pale, blue lightning shone upon the staring fronts of the houses.

By this time, too, every door was closed; but as Bob trudged homeward, his eye mechanically sought the public-house which had once belonged to Phil Slaney. A faint light was making its way through the shutters and the glass panes over the door-way, which made a sort of dull, foggy, halo about the front of the house.

As Bob's eyes had become accustomed to the obscurity by this time, the light in question was quite sufficient to enable him to see a man in a sort of loose riding-coat seated upon a bench, which, at that time, was fixed under the window of the house. He wore his hat very much over his eyes, and was smoking a long pipe. The outline of a glass and a quart bottle were also dimly traceable beside him; and a large horse saddled, but faintly discernible, was patiently awaiting his master's leisure.

There was something odd, no doubt, in the appearance of a traveller refreshing himself at such an hour in the open street; but the sexton accounted for it easily by supposing that, on the closing of the house for the night, he had taken what remained of his refection to the place where he was now discussing it al fresco.

At another time Bob might have saluted the stranger as he passed with a friendly 'good night'; but somehow, he was out of humour and in no genial mood, and was about passing without any courtesy of the sort, when the stranger, without taking the pipe from his mouth, raised the bottle, and with it beckoned him familiarly, while, with a sort of lurch of the head and shoulders, and at the same time shifting his seat to the end of the bench, he pantomimically invited him to share his seat and his cheer. There was a divine fragrance of whiskey about the spot, and Bob half relented; but he remembered his promise just as he began to waver, and said:

'No, I thank you, sir, I can't stop tonight.'

The stranger beckoned with vehement welcome, and pointed to the vacant space on the seat beside him.

'I thank you for your polite offer,' said Bob, 'but it's what I'm too late as it is, and haven't time to spare, so I wish you a good night.'

The traveller jingled the glass against the neck of the bottle, as if to intimate that he might at least swallow a dram without losing time. Bob was mentally quite of the same opinion; but, though his mouth watered, he remembered his promise, and shaking his head with incorruptible resolution, walked on.

The stranger, pipe in mouth, rose from his bench, the bottle in one hand, and the glass in the other, and followed at the sexton's heels, his dusky horse keeping close in his wake.

There was something suspicious and unaccountable in this importunity.

Bob quickened his pace, but the stranger followed close. The sexton began to feel queer, and turned about. His pursuer was behind, and still inviting him with impatient gestures to taste his liquor.

'I told you before,' said Bob, who was both angry and frightened, 'that I would not taste it, and that's enough. I don't want to have anything to say to you or your bottle; and in God's name,' he added, more vehemently, observing that he was approaching still closer, 'fall back and don't be tormenting me in this way.'

These words, as it seemed, incensed the stranger, for he shook the bottle with violent menace at Bob Martin, but, notwithstanding this gesture of defiance,

'The stranger beckoned with vehement welcome, and pointed to the vacant space on the seat beside him.'

he suffered the distance between them to increase. Bob, however, beheld him dogging him still in the distance, for his pipe shed a wonderful red glow, which duskily illuminated his entire figure like the lurid atmosphere of a meteor.

'I wish the devil had his own, my boy,' muttered the excited sexton, 'and I know well enough where you'd be.'

The next time he looked over his shoulder, to his dismay he observed the importunate stranger as close as ever upon his track.

'Confound you,' cried the man of skulls and shovels, almost beside himself with rage and horror, 'what is it you want of me?'

The stranger appeared more confident, and kept wagging his head and extending both glass and bottle toward him as he drew near, and Bob Martin heard the horse snorting as it followed in the dark.

'Keep it to yourself, whatever it is, for there is neither grace nor luck about you,' cried Bob Martin, freezing with terror; 'leave me alone, will you.'

And he fumbled in vain among the seething confusion of his ideas for a prayer or an exorcism. He quickened his pace almost to a run; he was now close to his own door, under the impending bank by the river side.

'Let me in, let me in, for God's sake; Molly, open the door,' he cried, as he ran to the threshold, and leant his back against the plank. His pursuer confronted him upon the road; the pipe was no longer in his mouth, but the dusky red glow still lingered around him. He uttered some inarticulate cavernous sounds, which were wolfish and indescribable, while he seemed employed in pouring out a glass from the bottle.

The sexton kicked with all his force against the door, and cried at the same time with a despairing voice.

'In the name of God Almighty, once for all, leave me alone.'

His pursuer furiously flung the contents of the bottle at Bob Martin; but instead of fluid it issued out in a stream of flame, which expanded and whirled round them, and for a moment they were both enveloped in a faint blaze; at the same instant a sudden gust whisked off the stranger's hat, and the sexton beheld that his skull was roofless. For an instant he beheld the gaping aperture, black and shattered, and then he fell senseless into his own doorway, which his affrighted wife had just unbarred.

I need hardly give my reader the key to this most intelligible and authentic narrative. The traveller was acknowledged by all to have been the spectre of the suicide, called up by the Evil One to tempt the convivial sexton into a violation of his promise, sealed, as it was, by an imprecation. Had he succeeded, no doubt the dusky steed, which Bob had seen saddled in attendance, was destined to have carried back a double burden to the place from whence he came.

As an attestation of the reality of this visitation, the old thorn tree which overhung the doorway was found in the morning to have been blasted with the infernal fires which had issued from the bottle, just as if a thunder-bolt had scorched it.

The moral of the above tale is upon the surface, apparent, and, so to speak, self-acting – a circumstance which happily obviates the necessity of our discussing it together. Taking our leave, therefore, of honest Bob Martin, who now sleeps soundly in the same solemn dormitory where, in his day, he made so many beds for others, I come to a legend of the Royal Irish Artillery, whose headquarters were for so long a time in the town of Chapelizod. I don't mean to say that I cannot tell a great many more stories, equally authentic and marvellous, touching this old town; but as I may possibly have to perform a like office for other localities, and as Anthony Poplar is known, like Atropos, to carry a shears, wherewith to snip across all 'yarns' which exceed reasonable bounds, I consider it, on the whole, safer to despatch the traditions of Chapelizod with one tale more.

Let me, however, first give it a name; for an author can no more despatch a tale without a title, than an apothecary can deliver his physic without a label. We shall, therefore, call it –

THE SPECTRE LOVERS

There lived some fifteen years since in a small and ruinous house, little better than a hovel, an old woman who was reported to have considerably exceeded her eightieth year, and who rejoiced in the name of Alice, or popularly, Ally Moran. Her society was not much courted, for she was neither rich, nor, as the reader may suppose, beautiful. In addition to a lean cur and a cat she had one human companion, her grandson, Peter Brien, whom, with laudable good nature, she had supported from the period of his orphanage down to that of my story, which finds him in his twentieth year. Peter was a good-natured slob of a fellow, much more addicted to wrestling, dancing, and love-making, than to hard work, and fonder of whiskey-punch than good advice. His grandmother had a high opinion of his accomplishments, which indeed was but natural, and also of his genius, for Peter had of late years begun to apply his mind to politics; and as it was plain that he had a mortal hatred of honest labour, his grandmother predicted, like a true fortune-teller, that he was born to marry an heiress, and Peter himself (who had no mind to forego his freedom even on such terms) that he was destined to find a pot of gold. Upon one point both agreed, that being unfitted by the peculiar bias of his genius for work, he was to acquire the immense fortune to which his merits entitled him by means of a pure run of good luck. This solution of Peter's future had the double effect of reconciling both himself and his grandmother to his idle courses, and also of maintaining that even flow of hilarious spirits which made him everywhere welcome, and which was in truth the natural result of his consciousness of approaching affluence.

It happened one night that Peter had enjoyed himself to a very late hour with two or three choice spirits near Palmerstown. They had talked politics and love, sung songs, and told stories, and, above all, had swallowed, in the chastened disguise of punch, at least a pint of good whiskey, every man.

It was considerably past one o'clock when Peter bid his companions goodbye, with a sigh and a hiccough, and lighting his pipe set forth on his solitary homeward way.

The bridge of Chapelizod was pretty nearly the midway point of his night march, and from one cause or another his progress was rather slow, and it was past two o'clock by the time he found himself leaning over its old battlements, and looking up the river, over whose winding current and wooded banks the soft moonlight was falling.

The cold breeze that blew lightly down the stream was grateful to him. It cooled his throbbing head, and he drank it in at his hot lips. The scene, too, had, without his being well sensible of it, a secret fascination. The village was sunk in the profoundest slumber, not a mortal stirring, not a sound afloat, a soft haze covered it all, and the fairy moonlight hovered over the entire landscape.

In a state between rumination and rapture, Peter continued to lean over the battlements of the old bridge, and as he did so he saw, or fancied he saw, emerging one after another along the river bank in the little gardens and enclosures in the rear of the street of Chapelizod, the queerest little white-washed huts and cabins he had ever seen there before. They had not been there that evening when he passed the bridge on the way to his merry tryst. But the most remarkable thing about it was the odd way in which these quaint little cabins showed themselves. First he saw one or two of them just with the corner of his eye, and when he looked full at them, strange to say, they faded away and disappeared. Then another and another came in view, but all in the same coy way, just appearing and gone again before he could well fix his gaze upon them; in a little while, however, they began to bear a fuller gaze, and he found, as it seemed to himself, that he was able by an effort of attention to fix the vision for a longer and longer time, and when they waxed faint and nearly vanished, he had the power of recalling them into light and substance, until at last their vacillating indistinctness became less and less, and they assumed a permanent place in the moonlit landscape.

'Be the hokey,' said Peter, lost in amazement, and dropping his pipe into the river unconsciously, 'them is the quarist bits iv mud cabins I ever seen, growing up like musharoons in the dew of an evening, and poppin' up here and down again there, and up again in another place like so many white rabbits in a warren; and there they stand at last as firm and fast as if they were there from the Deluge; bedad it's enough to make a man a'most believe in the fairies.'

This latter was a large concession from Peter, who was a bit of a free-thinker, and spoke contemptuously in his ordinary conversation of that class of agencies.

Having treated himself to a long last stare at these mysterious fabrics, Peter prepared to pursue his homeward way; having crossed the bridge and passed the mill, he arrived at the corner of the main-street of the little town, and casting a careless look up the Dublin road, his eye was arrested by a most unexpected spectacle.

This was no other than a column of foot soldiers, marching with perfect regularity towards the village, and headed by an officer on horseback. They were at the far side of the turnpike, which was closed; but much to his perplexity he perceived that they marched on through it without appearing to sustain the least check from that barrier.

On they came at a slow march; and what was most singular in the matter was, that they were drawing several cannons along with them; some held ropes, others spoked the wheels, and others again marched in front of the guns and behind them, with muskets shouldered, giving a stately character of parade and regularity to this, as it seemed to Peter, most unmilitary procedure.

It was owing either to some temporary defect in Peter's vision, or to some illusion attendant upon mist and moonlight, or perhaps to some other cause, that the whole procession had a certain waving and vapoury character which perplexed and tasked his eyes not a little. It was like the pictured pageant of a phantasmagoria reflected upon smoke. It was as if every breath disturbed it; sometimes it was blurred, sometimes obliterated; now here, now there. Sometimes, while the upper part was quite distinct, the legs of the column

'It was like the pictured pageant of a phantasmagoria reflected upon smoke.'

would nearly fade away or vanish outright, and then again they would come out into clear relief, marching on with measured tread, while the cocked hats and shoulders grew, as it were, transparent, and all but disappeared.

Notwithstanding these strange optical fluctuations, however, the column continued steadily to advance. Peter crossed the street from the corner near the old bridge, running on tip-toe, and with his body stooped to avoid observation, and took up a position upon the raised footpath in the shadow of the houses, where, as the soldiers kept the middle of the road, he calculated that he might, himself undetected, see them distinctly enough as they passed.

'What the div – , what on airth,' he muttered, checking the irreligious ejaculation with which he was about to start, for certain queer misgivings were hovering about his heart, notwithstanding the factitious courage of the whiskey bottle. 'What on airth is the manin' of all this? Is it the French that's landed at last to give us a hand and help us in airnest to this blessed repale? If it is not them, I simply ask who the div – , I mane who on airth are they, for such sogers as them I never seen before in my born days?'

By this time the foremost of them were quite near, and truth to say, they were the queerest soldiers he had ever seen in the course of his life. They wore long gaiters and leather breeches, three-cornered hats, bound with silver lace, long blue coats, with scarlet facings and linings, which latter were shewn by a fastening which held together the two opposite corners of the skirt behind; and in front the breasts were in like manner connected at a single point, where and below which they sloped back, disclosing a long-flapped waistcoat of snowy whiteness; they had very large, long cross-belts, and wore enormous pouches of white leather hung extraordinarily low, and on each of which a little silver star was glittering. But what struck him as most grotesque and outlandish in their costume was their extraordinary display of shirt-frill in front, and of ruffle about their wrists, and the strange manner in which their hair was frizzled out and powdered under their hats, and clubbed up into great rolls behind. But one of the party was mounted. He rode a tall white horse, with high action and arching neck; he had a snow-white feather in his three-cornered hat, and his coat was shimmering all over with a profusion of silver lace. From these circumstances Peter concluded that he must be the commander of the detachment, and examined him as he passed attentively. He was a slight, tall man, whose legs did not half fill his leather breeches, and he appeared to be at the wrong side of sixty. He had a shrunken, weather-beaten, mulberry coloured face, carried a large black patch over one eye, and turned neither to the right nor to the left, but rode on at the head of his men, with a grim, military, inflexibility.

The countenances of these soldiers, officers as well as men, seemed all full of trouble, and, so to speak, scared and wild. He watched in vain for a single contented or comely face. They had, one and all, a melancholy and hang-dog look; and as they passed by, Peter fancied that the air grew cold and thrilling.

He had seated himself upon a stone bench, from which, staring with all his might, he gazed upon the grotesque and noiseless procession as it filed by him. Noiseless it was; he could neither hear the jingle of accoutrements, the tread of feet, nor the rumble of the wheels; and when the old colonel turned his horse a little, and made as though he were giving the word of command, and a trumpeter, with a swollen blue nose and white feather fringe round his hat, who was walking beside him, turned about and put his bugle to his lips, still Peter heard nothing, although it was plain the sound had reached the soldiers, for they instantly changed their front to three abreast.

'Botheration!' muttered Peter, 'is it deaf I'm growing?'

But that could not be, for he heard the sighing of the breeze and the rush of the neighbouring Liffey plain enough.

'Well,' said he, in the same cautious key, 'by the piper, this bangs Banagher fairly! It's either the French army that's in it, come to take the town iv Chapelizod by surprise, an' makin' no noise for feard iv wakenin' the inhabitants; or else it's – it's – what it's – somethin' else. But, tundher-an-ouns, what's gone wid Fitzpatrick's shop across the way?'

The brown, dingy stone building at the opposite side of the street looked newer and cleaner than he had been used to see it; the front door of it stood open, and a sentry, in the same grotesque uniform, with shouldered musket, was pacing noiselessly to and fro before it. At the angle of this building, in like manner, a wide gate (of which Peter had no recollection whatever) stood open, before which, also, a similar sentry was gliding, and into this gateway the whole column gradually passed, and Peter finally lost sight of it.

'I'm not asleep; I'm not dhramin',' said he, rubbing his eyes, and stamping slightly on the pavement, to assure himself that he was wide awake. 'It is a quare business, whatever it is; an' it's not alone that, but everything about town looks strange to me. There's Tresham's house new painted, bedad, an' them flowers in the windies! An' Delany's house, too, that had not a whole pane of glass in it this morning, and scarce a slate on the roof of it! It is not possible it's what it's dhrunk I am. Sure there's the big tree, and not a leaf of it changed since I passed, and the stars overhead, all right. I don't think it is in my eyes it is.'

And so looking about him, and every moment finding or fancying new food for wonder, he walked along the pavement, intending, without further delay, to make his way home.

But his adventures for the night were not concluded. He had nearly reached the angle of the short land that leads up to the church, when for the first time he perceived that an officer, in the uniform he had just seen, was walking before, only a few yards in advance of him.

The officer was walking along at an easy, swinging gait, and carried his sword under his arm, and was looking down on the pavement with an air of reverie.

In the very fact that he seemed unconscious of Peter's presence, and disposed to keep his reflections to himself, there was something reassuring. Besides, the reader must please to remember that our hero had a quantum sufficit of good punch before his adventure commenced, and was thus fortified against those qualms and terrors under which, in a more reasonable state of mind, he might not impossibly have sunk.

The idea of the French invasion revived in full power in Peter's fuddled imagination, as he pursued the nonchalant swagger of the officer.

'Be the powers iv Moll Kelly, I'll ax him what it is,' said Peter, with a sudden accession of rashness. 'He may tell me or not, as he plases, but he can't be offinded, anyhow.'

With this reflection having inspired himself, Peter cleared his voice and began –

'Captain!' said he, 'I ax your pardon, captain, an' maybe you'd be so condescindin' to my ignorance as to tell me, if it's plasin' to yer honour, whether your honour is not a Frinchman, if it's plaisin to you.'

This he asked, not thinking that, had it been as he suspected, not one word of his question in all probability would have been intelligible to the person he addressed. He was, however, understood, for the officer answered him in English, at the same time slackening his pace and moving a little to the side of the pathway, as if to invite his interrogator to take his place beside him.

'No; I am an Irishman,' he answered.

'I humbly thank your honour,' said Peter, drawing nearer – for the affability and the nativity of the officer encouraged him – 'but maybe your honour is in the sarvice of the King of France?'

'I serve the same King as you do,' he answered, with a sorrowful significance which Peter did not comprehend at the time; and, interrogating in turn, he asked,

'But what calls you forth at this hour of the day?'

'The day, your honour! – the night, you mane.'

'It was always our way to turn night into day, and we keep to it still,' remarked the soldier. 'But, no matter, come up here to my house; I have a job for you, if you wish to earn some money easily. I live here.'

As he said this, he beckoned authoritatively to Peter, who followed almost mechanically at his heels, and they turned up a little lane near the old Roman Catholic chapel, at the end of which stood, in Peter's time, the ruins of a tall, stone-built house.

Like everything else in the town, it had suffered a metamorphosis. The stained and ragged walls were now erect, perfect, and covered with pebble-dash; window-panes glittered coldly in every window; the green hall-door had a bright brass knocker on it. Peter did not know whether to believe his previous or his present impressions; seeing is believing, and Peter could not dispute the reality of the scene. All the records of his memory seemed but the images of a tipsy dream. In a trance of astonishment and perplexity, therefore, he submitted himself to the chances of his adventure.

The door opened, the officer beckoned with a melancholy air of authority to Peter, and entered. Our hero followed him into a sort of hall, which was very dark, but he was guided by the steps of the soldier, and, in silence, they ascended the stairs. The moonlight, which shone in at the lobbies, showed an old, dark wainscoting, and a heavy, oak banister. They passed by closed doors at different landing-places, but all was dark and silent as, indeed, became that late hour of the night.

Now they ascended to the topmost floor. The captain paused for a minute at the nearest door, and, with a heavy groan, pushing it open, entered the room. Peter remained at the threshold. A slight female form in a sort of loose, white robe, and with a great deal of dark hair hanging loosely about her, was standing in the middle of the floor, with her back towards them.

The soldier stopped short before he reached her, and said, in a voice of great anguish, 'Still the same, sweet bird – sweet bird! Still the same.' Whereupon, she turned suddenly, and threw her arms about the neck of the officer, with a gesture of fondness and despair, and her frame was agitated as if by a burst of sobs. He held her close to his breast in silence; and honest Peter felt a strange terror creep over him, as he witnessed these mysterious sorrows and endearments.

'Tonight, tonight – and then ten years more – ten long years – another ten years.'

The officer and the lady seemed to speak these words together; her voice mingled with his in a musical and fearful wail, like a distant summer wind, in the dead hour of night, wandering through ruins. Then he head the officer say, alone, in a voice of anguish –

'Upon me be it all, for ever, sweet birdie, upon me.'

And again they seemed to mourn together in the same soft and desolate wail, like sounds of grief heard from a great distance.

Peter was thrilled with horror, but he was also under a strange fascination; and an intense and dreadful curiosity held him fast.

The moon was shining obliquely into the room, and through the window Peter saw the familiar slopes of the Park, sleeping mistily under its shimmer. He could also see the furniture of the room with tolerable distinctness – the old balloon-backed chairs, a four-post bed in a sort of recess, and a rack against the wall, from which hung some military clothes and accoutrements; and the sight of all these homely objects reassured him somewhat, and he could not help feeling unspeakably curious to see the face of the girl whose long hair was streaming over the officer's epaulet.

Peter, accordingly, coughed, at first slightly, and afterward more loudly, to recall her from her reverie of grief; and, apparently, he succeeded; for she turned round, as did her companion, and both, standing hand in hand gazed upon him fixedly. He thought he had never seen such large, strange eyes in all his life; and their gaze seemed to chill the very air around him, and arrest the pulses of his heart. An eternity of misery and remorse was in the shadowy faces that looked upon him.

If Peter had taken less whiskey by a single thimbleful, it is probable that he would have lost heart altogether before these figures, which seemed every moment to assume a more marked and fearful, though hardly definable, contrast to ordinary human shapes.

'What is it you want with me?' he stammered.

'To bring my lost treasure to the churchyard,' replied the lady, in a silvery voice of more than mortal desolation.

The word 'treasure' revived the resolution of Peter, although a cold sweat was covering him, and his hair was bristling with horror; he believed, however, that he was on the brink of fortune, if he could but command nerve to brave the interview to its close.

'And where,' he gasped, 'is it hid – where will I find it?'

They both pointed to the sill of the window, through which the moon was shining at the far end of the room, and the soldier said –

'Under that stone.'

Peter drew a long breath, and wiped the cold dew from his face, preparatory to passing to the window, where he expected to secure the reward of his protracted terrors. But looking steadfastly at the window, he saw the faint image of a new-born child sitting upon the sill in the moonlight, with its little arms stretched toward him, and a smile so heavenly as he never beheld before.

At the sight of this, strange to say, his heart entirely failed him, he looked on the figures that stood near, and beheld them gazing on the infantine form with a smile so guilty and distorted, that he felt as if he were entertaining alive among the scenery of hell, and shuddering, he cried in an irrepressible agony of horror –

'I'll have nothing to say with you, and nothing to do with you; I don't know what yez are or what yez want iv me, but let me go this minute, every one of yez, in the name of God.'

With these words there came a strange rumbling and sighing about Peter's ears; he lost sight of everything, and felt that peculiar and not unpleasant sensation of falling, softly, that sometimes supervenes in sleep, ending in a dull shock. After that he had neither dream nor consciousness till he wakened, chill and stiff, stretched between two piles of old rubbish, among the black and roofless walls of the ruined house.

We need hardly mention that the village had put on its wonted air of neglect and decay, or that Peter looked around him in vain for traces of those novelties which had so puzzled and distracted him upon the previous night.

'Ay, ay,' said his grandmother, removing her pipe, as he ended his description of the view from the bridge, 'sure enough I remember myself, when I was a slip of a girl, these little white cabins among the gardens by the river side. The artillery sogers that was married, or had not room in the barracks, used to be in them, but they're all gone long ago.

'The Lord be merciful to us!' she resumed, when he had described the military procession. 'It's often I seen the regiment marchin' into the town, jist as you saw it last night, acushla. Oh, voch, but it makes my heart sore to think iv them days; they were pleasant times, sure enough; but is not it terrible, avick, to think it's what it was the ghost of the rigiment you seen? The Lord betune us an' harm, for it was nothing else, as sure as I'm sittin' here.'

When he mentioned the peculiar physiognomy and figure of the old officer who rode at the head of the regiment –

'That,' said the old crone, dogmatically, 'was ould Colonel Grimshaw, the Lord presarve us! He's buried in the churchyard iv Chapelizod, and well I remember him, when I was a young thing, an' a cross ould floggin' fellow he was wid the men, an' a devil's boy among the girls – rest his soul!'

'Amen!' said Peter; 'it's often I read his tomb-stone myself; but he's a long time dead.'

'Sure, I tell you he died when I was no more nor a slip iv a girl – the Lord betune us and harm!'

'I'm afeard it is what I'm not long for this world myself, afther seeing such a sight as that,' said Peter, fearfully.

'Nonsinse, avourneen,' retorted his grandmother, indignantly, though she had herself misgivings on the subject; 'Sure there was Phil Doolan, the ferryman, that seen black Ann Scanlan in his own boat, and what harm ever kem of it?'

Peter proceeded with his narrative, but when he came to the description of the house, in which his adventure had had so sinister a conclusion, the old woman was at fault.

'I know the house and the ould walls well, an' I can remember the time there was a roof on it, and the doors an' windows in it, but it had a bad name about being haunted, but by who, or for what, I forget entirely.'

'Did you ever hear was there goold or silver there?' he inquired.

'No, no, avick, don't be thinking about the likes; take a fool's advice, and never go next to near them ugly black walls again the longest day you have to live; an' I'd take my davy, it's what it's the same word the priest himself id be afther sayin' to you if you wor to ax his raverence consarnin' it, for it's plain to be seen it was nothing good you seen there, and there's neither luck nor grace about it.'

Peter's adventure made no little noise in the neighbourhood, as the reader may well suppose; and a few evenings after it, being on an errand to old Major Vandeleur, who lived in a snug old-fashioned house, close by the river, under a perfect bower of ancient trees, he was called on to relate the story in the parlour.

The Major was, as I have said, an old man; he was small, lean, and upright, with a mahogany complexion, and a wooden inflexibility of face; he was a man, besides, of few words, and if he was old, it follows plainly that his mother was older still. Nobody could guess or tell how old, but it was admitted that her own generation had long passed away, and that she had not a competitor left. She had French blood in her veins, and although she did not retain her charms quite so well as Ninon de l'Enclos, she was in full possession of all her mental activity, and talked quite enough for herself and the Major.

'So, Peter,' she said, 'you have seen the dear, old Royal Irish again in the streets of Chapelizod. Make him a tumbler of punch, Frank; and Peter, sit down, and while you take it let us have the story.'

Peter accordingly, seated near the door, with a tumbler of the nectarian stimulant steaming beside him, proceeded with marvellous courage, considering they had no light but the uncertain glare of the fire, to relate with minute particularity his awful adventure. The old lady listened at first with a smile of good-natured incredulity; her cross-examination touching the drinking-bout at Palmerstown had been teazing, but as the narrative proceeded she became attentive, and at length absorbed, and once or twice she uttered ejaculations of pity or awe. When it was over, the old lady looked with somewhat sad and stern abstraction on the table, patting her cat assiduously meanwhile, and then suddenly looking upon her son, the Major, she said –

'Frank, as sure as I live he has seen the wicked Captain Devereux.'

The Major uttered an inarticulate expression of wonder.

'The house was precisely that he has described. I have told you the story often, as I heard it from your dear grandmother, about the poor young lady he ruined, and the dreadful suspicion about the little baby. She, poor thing, died in that house heart-broken, and you know he was shot shortly after in a duel.'

This was the only light that Peter ever received respecting his adventure. It was supposed, however, that he still clung to the hope that treasure of some sort was hidden about the old house, for he was often seen lurking about its walls, and at last his fate overtook him, poor fellow, in the pursuit, for climbing near the summit one day, his holding gave way, and he fell upon the hard uneven ground, fracturing a leg and a rib, and after a short interval died, and he, like the other heroes of these true tales, lies buried in the little churchyard of Chapelizod.

'Ghost Stories of Chapelizod' was first published in the Dublin University Magazine *in January 1851. It was reprinted in* Madam Crowl's Ghost and Other Tales of Mystery *in 1923.*

Ghastly Haunt Thy Native Place
Bram Stoker's Dublin

INTRODUCTION

The evolution of the literary vampire in English can be traced in three broad strides: 'The Vampyre' (1819) by Dr John Polidori, 'Carmilla' (1872) by Joseph Sheridan Le Fanu and the immediately recognisable *Dracula* (1897) by Bram Stoker.[82]

Bram Stoker (1847-1912), while not exactly a household name today, was quite well known in the England, Ireland and America of the late nineteenth century; though not for having written *Dracula*. His claim to fame was managing London's prestigious Lyceum Theatre owned by Sir Henry Irving, one of the most distinguished actors of the late Victorian period. Long before Stoker was known for his fiction, he was rubbing shoulders with the likes of Mark Twain, Alfred Lord Tennyson, Hall Caine[83], Richard Burton, Arthur Conan Doyle and the notorious Wilde family. An amateur writer, Stoker was hardly the type of man most would associate with that masterpiece of Victorian horror, *Dracula*.

Much of Stoker's fiction is not set in Ireland and, maybe not surprisingly, he is rarely considered an Irish writer. However, Stoker spent thirty-one years, nearly half of his life, in Dublin before moving to London in 1878. Stoker lived and worked in the arteries and veins of Dublin, the city's blood mingling with his. While his working notes do not state that Dublin directly inspired his seminal work *Dracula,* the influence of Ireland's eerie atmosphere was, and still is, unavoidable – and today scarlet traces can be found in Stoker's native Dublin soil.[84]

CLONTARF & ENVIRONS

MARINO CRESCENT

Childhood builds its own shrines; and these live untarnished and unimpaired to the end.

– from *The Man* (1905)

Abraham (Bram) Stoker was born on 8 November 1847 to Abraham and Charlotte (*née* Thornley) Stoker. Stoker's first two years of childhood were spent in a Georgian neighbourhood in Clontarf at 15 Marino Crescent. Bedridden from birth, Stoker was unable to walk, and remained an invalid until he was seven years old. Stoker's father Abraham was a civil servant at Dublin Castle, earning just enough to live comfortably with his wife and seven children. Stoker's mother Charlotte grew up in Sligo during the 1832-1834 cholera pandemic, where she experienced first-hand the horrors of the plague. Charlotte had a penchant for morbid mothering and spent much of her time infecting the bedridden Bram's imagination with gruesome stories of cholera victims and premature burials:

> One action I vividly remember. A poor traveler was taken ill on the roadside some miles from the town, and how did those samaritans tend him? They dug a pit and with long poles pushed him living into it, and covered him up quick, alive.[85]

The stories Charlotte told young Stoker are thought by many to have influenced his first book of fiction, *Under the Sunset* (1881), a collection of moralistic children's stories. Stories such as 'The Invisible Giant' were foreshadowed by Charlotte's grim reminiscences:

> [I]n many houses lay one, nay two or three dead. One house would be attacked and the next spared. There was no telling who would go next, and when one said goodbye to a friend he said it as if for ever.[86]

The cause of Stoker's illness is still unknown. Some scholars believe it was psychological, self-inflicted or an Oedipal complex, though it seems fairly obvious that Mrs Stoker's ghastly tales of nightly nihilism and bloated corpses were enough to scare any child into not leaving the safety and comfort of bed.

Marino Crescent is a picturesque semi-circle of Georgian houses facing Dublin Bay. Now known as 'The Crescent', Marino Crescent was in earlier times known as 'Spite Row'. Charles Ffolliott originally acquired the land in 1792 and intended to build upon it. Lord Charlemont, who owned the adjacent land, wanted to preserve his mansion's unspoiled view of the sea and discouraged

above left The Stoker Home, 15 Marino Crescent

above right The Balcombe Home, 1 Marino Crescent

Ffolliott by charging outrageous taxes on building supplies at a tollgate on his land. Ffolliott not only avoided the toll by hiring a barge to transport supplies across the harbour, but deliberately built Marino Crescent so as to block Lord Charlemont's view of Dublin Bay.

The Stoker family moved from Marino Crescent in late 1849 to Artane Lodge in nearby Artane where they stayed for the remainder of Stoker's early childhood.[87]

In 1876, twenty-seven years after the Stokers moved from number 15 Marino Crescent, the recently retired Lieutenant-Colonel James Balcombe moved his family into 1 Marino Crescent. Lieutenant-Colonel Balcombe's daughter, Florence Ann Lemon Balcombe, one-time love-interest of Oscar Wilde, would become Bram Stoker's future wife. Oscar Wilde described Florence as, 'exquisitely pretty...just seventeen with the most perfectly beautiful face I ever saw and not a sixpence of money.'[88]

The Balcombe home is more extravagant than the Stokers' residence. Curiously enough, it now seems to be the offices of estate agents. One cannot help but think of another estate agent, Jonathan Harker, as he precariously made his way towards Castle Dracula.

Like many Georgian neighbourhoods, a beautiful park forms the centrepiece of The Crescent. The park is surprisingly quiet for being so close to the relatively busy Clontarf Road. Any Stoker-enthusiast will want to pause here, if not for the peacefulness of the park, then for the small wooden kiosk that stands in front of the Stoker house.

The kiosk presents information on Bram Stoker's life; a stand-in for the explanatory plaques normally affixed to historical landmarks, but is absent from Stoker's birthplace. Displayed on the kiosk are photographs of Bram, his parents Abraham and Charlotte, his wife Florence and his only son Noel. There is also a short, two-page biography and three facsimiles from the original typesetter's manuscript for *Dracula*. One page includes a paragraph excised from the novel in which Castle Dracula is destroyed in a rather spectacular Poe-like manner by rampant forces of nature.[89]

SAINT JOHN THE BAPTIST'S CHURCHYARD

> Then I too moved, but I had to go round headstones and railed-off tombs, and I stumbled over graves. The sky was overcast, and somewhere far off an early cock crew. A little ways off, beyond a line of scattered juniper trees, which marked the pathway to the church, a white dim figure flitted in the direction of the tomb.
>
> – from *Dracula* (1897)

Not far from Marino Crescent is Saint John the Baptist's churchyard. Young Stoker was baptised and christened in Saint John's on 30 December 1847. The church, which lies in the shadow of Clontarf Castle, is now a ruin, and, on a grey day, has the most intensely gothic atmosphere this side of Whitby.

Entering through the small gates on Castle Avenue, the first thing you will see is a roofless church centred in the yard. The remains stand stoically under a skin of ivy that has long covered the church's old stone bones. Tombstones cram the yard and are often illegible, as many are overgrown in tangles of weeds. The churchyard, an oasis of moodiness in Clontarf, is worth the quick out-of-the-way jaunt to visit.

Saint John the Baptist's Churchyard

On your way to Saint John's you may wish to take a quick peek at Clontarf Castle, just around the corner on Castle Avenue. The castle as it stands today dates back to 1837. The previous castle dates back to 1172. Both the church and castle were connected with the legendary Knights Templar until Pope Clement V outlawed the order for heresy in 1307. On the grounds of the castle, visitors will find remnants of the medieval sect in the form of The Knight's Bar and The Templar Bistro. As for the castle itself, it has been transformed into the ultimate tourist attraction: an expensive four-star hotel aptly enough called The Clontarf Castle Hotel.

THE BRAM STOKER DRACULA EXPERIENCE

The Bram Stoker Dracula Experience is across the street from Marino Crescent. Absurdly, the museum is housed in the same building as an ultra-hip fitness club, one that would look more at home in Los Angeles than in a north Dublin suburb. The museum, which opened in the spring of 2003, is a welcome addition to Dublin's long list of literary tourist attractions. The exhibit begins with a long corridor filled with an illustrated biography of Stoker's life using reproductions of photographs and personal documents. From there, the museum turns into a carnival-like funhouse taking you through Dracula's castle, and placing you face to face with the Count himself. The museum also boasts two slick mini-cinemas, one showing a video presentation on Stoker, and the other usually a cinematic adaptation of *Dracula*.

For lunch you might wish to visit Bram's Café (+353 1 833 5610) at 4 St Aidan's Road, just across Clontarf Road from Marino Crescent. However, Bram's Café is Stoker-themed in name and menu only, serving dishes like Bram's Burger, Bram's B.L.T., Bram's Breakfast and Bram's Vegetarian Club Sandwich.

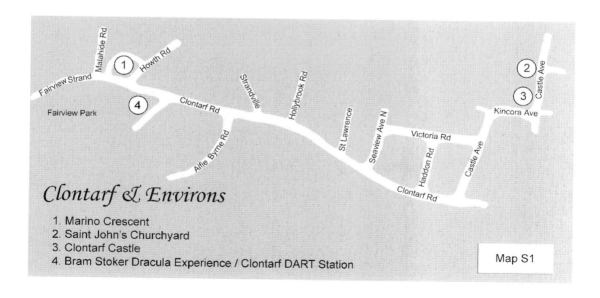

Clontarf & Environs

1. Marino Crescent
2. Saint John's Churchyard
3. Clontarf Castle
4. Bram Stoker Dracula Experience / Clontarf DART Station

Map S1

How to Get There

The Stoker landmarks in Clontarf are relatively easy to get to. The Dublin Area Rapid Transit (DART) has a station on Clontarf Road, practically across the street from The Crescent and next door to the Bram Stoker Dracula Experience (+353 1 805 7824). The museum is in the West Wood Club and accessed through Bar Code, an adjoining bar at the rear of the building. Saint John's churchyard is on Castle Avenue, a bit of a hike from Marino Crescent, though a pleasant suburban stroll. While in Clontarf you may also want to consider paying a visit to the infamous Casino Marino, the opulent garden pavilion built for the bested Lord Charlemont.

NORTH CITY CENTRE

BECTIVE HOUSE COLLEGE

[Dracula] dared even to attend the Scholomance...amongst the mountains over Lake Hermanstadt, where the devil claims the tenth scholar as his due...and there was no branch of knowledge of his time that he did not essay.

– from *Dracula* (1897)

From 1858 until 1864 the Stoker family lived at 17 Buckingham Road Upper, near Connolly Station, now replaced by a strip of Dublin Corporation housing. During this time, Stoker overcame his mysterious childhood illness and was well enough to attend Bective House College, then run by Dr John Lardner Burke.[90] Here Stoker was primed to attend Dublin's bastion of education, Trinity College. Of course neither Bective House College nor Trinity taught courses half as diabolical as those taught at Scholomance, Dracula's *alma mater*.

Bective House College stood near the north-east corner where Parnell Square East meets Gardiner Row.[91]

Stoker's paternal uncles, Edward Alexander and William, were both noted physicians and had connections with Dublin's prestigious Royal College of Surgeons. Indeed, Stoker's entire family had a history in the medical field, including his grandfather, William, and three of his brothers, Richard, George and Sir William Thornley.[92] 'Doubtless measles ran its course through Bram's household, and Uncle William would have bled him and his brothers and sisters by attaching leeches to the skin.'[93] If Stoker did endure such an experience it must have left an indelible mark on his imagination, as vivid and as blood-red as the puncture wounds on Lucy Westenra's pale neck.

The move to 17 Buckingham Road Upper, near Connolly Station placed the Stoker family closer to Edward Alexander Stoker, who lived at 49 Parnell Square. Number 49 Parnell Square was, until only recently, a large hole in the ground at the corner of Parnell Square West and Granby Place.

The Children of Lir

Admittedly, there is little on Parnell Square still standing that directly relates to Bram Stoker's life. However, it should be pointed out that the beautiful Garden of Remembrance, in the centre of Parnell Square, is an excellent place to sit and eat lunch before venturing into the Dublin Writers Museum on the north side of the square. The garden commemorates the people who gave their lives for Ireland's independence, and features a massive sculpture by Oisín Kelly depicting the popular Irish legend of the Children of Lir.

DUBLIN WRITERS MUSEUM

The Dublin Writers Museum is a nice museum with a comfortable café and bookshop located at the rear, fully stocked with Irish literature. Unfortunately, the displays give little weight to the Irish masters of the ghostly and supernatural.

Maturin, Le Fanu and Stoker are given a small display case to share. Even the celebrated Oscar Wilde does not get a very grand treatment due to the museum's space constrictions.

Amongst the Stoker paraphernalia on display are an abridged 1901 paperback edition of *Dracula* with the classic cartoon cover of the Count climbing headfirst down the wall of the castle[94], a first edition of *Under the Sunset* and an autographed letter from Bram to journalist William Courtney dated 27 July 1883 that reads, rather uninterestingly, 'I am glad to say we have two seats for you...will you breakfast with us at Covent Garden Hotel...'

Upstairs in the museum's library a set of first edition books by Stoker and other Irish writers can be found. Of Stoker's eighteen published books, a good many of which are still in print, only *Dracula* is available in the otherwise well-stocked bookshop on the ground floor.

Another item of interest, in addition to the typewriter that Brendan Behan supposedly hurled through a pub window, is a small and unassuming chair that G.F. Handel graced with his bum when he debuted *The Messiah* in Dublin on 13 April 1742. We shall return briefly to Handel towards the end of this tour.

How to Get There

Parnell Square is relatively easy to get to provided that you do not set off from Sackville Street looking for Rutland Square. Parnell Square is at the north tip of O'Connell Street and is an easy walk from there. The Dublin Writers Museum (+353 1 872 2077) is located on the north side at 18 Parnell Square. (For a map of Parnell Square, see Map L1 – Dominick Street & Environs, page 57.)

TRINITY COLLEGE & ENVIRONS

TRINITY COLLEGE

In my babyhood I used, I understand, to be often at the point of death. Certainly till I was about seven years old I never knew what it was to stand upright...This early weakness, however, passed away in time and I grew into a strong boy and in time enlarged into the biggest member of my family...I was physically immensely strong.

– from *Personal Reminiscences of Henry Irving* (1906)

By the time Stoker entered Trinity College in 1864 at the age of seventeen, he was well known for his robust athleticism and towering stature. At 6'2" (1.88 m), 175 lbs, (79 kg) and with a full head of striking, ginger-coloured hair, the physically imposing Stoker seemed determined to make up for the time he had lost as an invalid.[95] Young Bram 'threw himself tenaciously into the social and sporting sides of undergraduate life.'[96] Much like today's college students, students of Bram's time prioritised extracurricular activities and Bram could often be found in the local pubs or the always-fashionable Bewley's Oriental Café, now located on Grafton Street.[97]

Stoker won an astounding number of awards for athleticism. 'He made the rugby team, was an oarsman, and excelled in long-distance walking events. As University Athlete in 1867, he won awards for weight lifting and the five- and seven-mile walks.'[98]

It was also during his time at Trinity that Stoker first showed literary tendencies. He was elected president of the Philosophical Society and held the position of auditor in the Historical Society, being one of the few people to simultaneously hold both positions. Most important was his fondness for the disreputable poet Walt Whitman (1819-1892), whose discovery is best described in Stoker's own words:

> One day I met a man in the Quad who had a copy [of *Leaves of Grass*], and I asked him to let me look at it. He acquiesced readily: 'Take the damn thing,' he said; 'I've had enough of it!' I took the book with me into the Park and in the shade of an elm tree began to read it.[99]

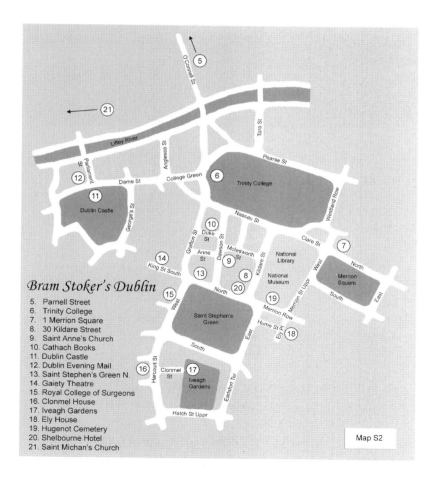

Bram Stoker's Dublin

5. Parnell Street
6. Trinity College
7. 1 Merrion Square
8. 30 Kildare Street
9. Saint Anne's Church
10. Cathach Books
11. Dublin Castle
12. Dublin Evening Mail
13. Saint Stephen's Green N.
14. Gaiety Theatre
15. Royal College of Surgeons
16. Clonmel House
17. Iveagh Gardens
18. Ely House
19. Hugenot Cemetery
20. Shelbourne Hotel
21. Saint Michan's Church

Map S2

Trinity College

A quiet park in Trinity College

Stoker, along with a few other academics, defended the then much-maligned American poet against Trinity's literary establishment. He identified with Whitman's barbaric yawp and entered into a brief correspondence with the elderly poet. He would later meet Whitman on three occasions during his many trips to America.

Stoker graduated from Trinity in 1871 with a bachelor's degree in science, which he supplemented with a master's degree in 1875.

Trinity College is located in the centre of Dublin, just south of the Liffey River. The college was founded in 1592 during the reign of Queen Elizabeth I, though most of the present buildings date to the mid-eighteenth century. Trinity's collection of cobblestone courtyards, stately buildings and world-famous library, which now houses the majority of Stoker's personal and family papers, should all be toured in full to be truly appreciated.

While the exact tree under which Stoker discovered Whitman is unknown, there are plenty of parks and quadrangles with elm trees under which to sit and discover both Whitman and Stoker. (For more on Trinity College, see pages 16 and 62.)

If you leave Trinity by the south entrance on Nassau Street, you will be at the corner of Nassau and Dawson Street. The site where Eason's Bookshop presently stands was, in Stoker's time, the Morrison Hotel, whose pub was utilised for the Historical Society's meetings. There is an abnormal amount of bookshops on Dawson Street, making this an excellent place to pause for book shopping.

1 MERRION SQUARE

'I am still puzzled to know why [the cat] is so keen against that mummy
...there are, I suppose, a lot of them. I saw three in the hall as I came in.'
   'There are lots of them,' she answered, 'I sometimes don't know whether I am in
a private house or the British Museum!'

– from *The Jewel of Seven Stars* (1903)

Continue along the south side of Trinity, down Nassau Street heading eastwards, and you will eventually end up on Merrion Square, the loveliest and most impressive of Dublin's famous Georgian squares. On the near corner is 1 Merrion Square, home of Sir William and Lady Jane Wilde, parents of the ubiquitous Oscar Wilde.

The Wildes' house may not have been filled with artefacts of exotic Egyptian antiquity, as suggested in the above quote, but every Saturday night the house filled with exotics, eccentrics and bohemians for weekly social gatherings hosted by the idiosyncratic Lady Jane Wilde, where Stoker 'breathed in the latest cultural and political crosscurrents.'[100]

Sir William Wilde, in addition to being a prominent ear and eye doctor, was a noted Egyptologist who took part in an exploration of Egypt in 1838, during which he acquired a mummified dwarf as a souvenir.[101] It is conceivable that

The Wilde Home,
1 Merrion Square

during one of these gatherings the fashionable topic of Egyptology arose. The stories of ancient and wind-swept Egypt, as related to Stoker by Sir William, were almost certainly a contributing influence on the former's novel of an Egyptian mummy's revenge, *The Jewel of Seven Stars* (1903).

While reading Stoker's *The Jewel of Seven Stars*, one can easily transpose the setting from a Kensington house in London to the Wilde's Merrion Square home in Dublin; casting Sir William as the Egyptologist Mr Trelawney, and Stoker as the intrepid solicitor Mr Malcolm Ross, as they solve the horrifying mystery of Queen Tera's mummy. (For more on Merrion Square, see page 65.)

The Wildes became surrogate parents to Stoker when his own parents left to live on the Continent in 1870. They had a strong interest in Irish legends, myths, and folklore, on which Sir William wrote numerous books.[102] Through the Wildes, Stoker would have been exposed to tales of the *dearg due* (an Irish blood-sucking demon), and come across the phrase '*droch fhúil*' which is Irish for 'bad blood' and uncannily pronounced 'druck ill'. Needless to say, many of those who have written about the origins of *Dracula* seize upon this homophone.[103]

Those with a little extra time on their hands may wish to pop across the street to the corner of Merrion Park, opposite 1 Merrion Square, where Oscar himself can be found, reclining on a rock, awaiting admirers.

THE KILDARE STREET CLUB

Backtracking slightly, to the corner of Leinster Street and Kildare Street, you will find the former meetinghouse of the Kildare Street Club. The Kildare Street Club once occupied 1-2 Kildare Street. It reached the height of its popularity during Stoker's lifetime and boasted numerous Dublin notables as members. The most curious features of the building are the carvings of animals and musical instruments found at the base of the pillars between the windows. The strangest is, perhaps, a trio of malnourished monkeys playing billiards. While this has little to do with Stoker, the monkeys look sinister enough to be the companions of the simian-demon that haunted the Reverend Mr Jennings in Joseph Sheridan Le Fanu's weird tale 'Green Tea' (1869).

Le Fanu, a ghost story writer and newspaper magnate, may have had another, more direct influence on young Stoker. Le Fanu's novella 'Carmilla' (1872) is the story of Countess Karnstein, a vampire who haunts a young girl in Styria, Austria. Stoker was undoubtedly aware of Le Fanu's work, as Le Fanu was somewhat of an omnipresent entity in Dublin at the time. Stoker's own short story, 'Dracula's Guest' (1914), thought by some to be an excised chapter from *Dracula*,[104] is also set in Styria, and features Countess Dolingen of Gratz, 'a beautiful woman with rounded cheeks and red lips.'[105]

It has also been posited that Abraham Van Helsing, the fearless Dutch doctor in *Dracula*, was inspired, in both name and profession, by Le Fanu's German physician Dr Martin Hesselius, both men being well-trained in the fields of

The billiard-playing monkeys of Kildare Street

medicine and metaphysics.[106] The long shadow that Joseph Sheridan Le Fanu cast over Bram Stoker should not be underestimated.

The Kildare Street Club was founded in 1782 and had its original meeting house on the present day site of the Royal Physician's Society, also on Kildare Street. The building was destroyed in a fire in 1860 and the club moved to 1-2 Kildare Street. Unfortunately, what was once known as Dublin's finest nineteenth-century interior was gutted to make room for the present occupants of the building: the National Heraldic Museum of Ireland, the National Genealogical Office and Alliance Française.

A touch off-topic, but no less interesting is that Club, a tasty orange-flavoured beverage, readily found in convenience stores throughout Ireland, got its name from the Kildare Street Club.[107]

30 KILDARE STREET

> I long to go through the crowded streets of your mighty London, to be in the midst of the whirl and rush of humanity, to share its life, its change, its death, and all that makes it what it is.
>
> – from *Dracula* (1897)

Continuing southward on Kildare Street, you will find one of the only remaining houses in the city centre inhabited by Stoker. Being something of a drifter, Stoker moved in and out of his brother Thornley's house on Harcourt Street and temporary dwellings on Kildare, Baggot and Leeson Street. When the Stoker family moved to the Continent in 1872, Bram moved to Cunningham's Lodge at 30 Kildare Street, his first independent address.[108]

Cunningham's Lodge catered to young and unmarried gentlemen like Bram, and is, conveniently for both Bram and sightseers, within walking distance of both the Wildes' home on Merrion Square and Thornley's home on Harcourt Street. Around this time, and much to his father's dismay, Stoker entertained the idea of moving to London 'to try his hand at full-time authorship' after recently having his first short story 'The Crystal Cup' (1872) published in *London Society*.[109]

Thirty Kildare Street is the only building in Ireland that Bram lived in to have a plaque affixed to it.

Cunningham Lodge is directly across the street from the National Library and the National Archaeology and History Museum of Ireland, two worthy, though unrelated stops along the Stoker trail. Both the library and museum have free exhibitions that are strongly recommended.

30 Kildare Street

Saint Anne's Church

SAINT ANNE'S CHURCH

From Kildare Street, cut back west along Molesworth Street to Dawson Street. Near the corner of Dawson and Molesworth sits Saint Anne's Church, one of Dublin's notable, central churches. Saint Anne's was built around 1720, with its striking Neo-Romanesque façade added by Sir Thomas Deane in 1868. The interior of the church has been altered little since its restoration in the 1860s and looks much as it did when Stoker was a parishioner there.

Saint Anne's Church is where Bram Stoker married Florence Balcombe, Oscar Wilde's former sweetheart, on 4 December 1878. Bram was thirty-one years old, Florence, or Florrie as she was affectionately known, was nineteen. They skipped the honeymoon, travelling immediately to England on business, and subsequently took up permanent residence in central London.

Little else is known of Bram and Florrie's courtship, save for the anecdote in which the spurned Oscar asked Florrie to return a small golden cross engraved with his name, even though he described the cross as a 'worthless trinket'. Florrie suggested that they meet at Stoker's residence on Harcourt Street. Oscar replied, '...quite out of the question; it would have been unfair to you, and me, and to the man you are going to marry....We should part where we first met' – the Balcombe home on Marino Crescent.[110]

The Stokers and Wildes, whose paths crossed numerous times in both Dublin and London, were all parishioners at Saint Anne's. The church is not only where Bram and Florrie wed, but also where Oscar Fingal O'Flahertie Wills Wilde was christened with his cumbersome name.

One block away, on nearby Duke Street, is Cathach Books, dealers of antique, out of print, and rare books of Irish interest. The tiny shop is neatly stocked with books from floor to ceiling. Signed volumes by Stoker, Joyce, Wilde and others can usually be found displayed on shelves and in glass cases, making the shop as much a museum as a business. Those with unlimited capital can unload their burden here.

How to Get There

Trinity College is one of Dublin's central landmarks and easy to find. Its main entrance is at the junction of College Green, College Street and Grafton Street, a five-minute walk from O'Connell Bridge.

One Merrion Square, which now houses the American College Dublin (+353 1 662 0281), is located at the west end of Merrion Square North and is open to the public for guided tours. Advance booking is essential.

The National Heraldic Museum (+353 1 661 8811) is located in the former Kildare Street Club building at 2-3 Kildare Street.

Stoker's residence at 30 Kildare Street is now privately owned and situated across the street from the National Library of Ireland (+353 1 603 0200) and the National Archaeology and History Museum of Ireland (+353 1 677 7444).

Saint Anne's Church (+353 1 676 7727) is on Dawson Street, and can be reached from Kildare Street via Molesworth Street.

Duke Street is one block north of Saint Anne's Church on Dawson Street. Cathach Books (+353 1 671 8676) is on the north side of Duke Street.

WEST CITY CENTRE

DUBLIN CASTLE

From age sixteen until his retirement fifty years later in 1865, Bram's father Abraham Stoker worked as a civil servant in the Chief Secretary's office at Dublin Castle. Shortly after his father's retirement, Stoker took the year off from college to work as a clerk for the Registrar of Petty Sessions. The job was most

Dublin Castle's Chapel Royal

The Dubhlinn Garden and
Stable House

likely taken at his father's insistence.[111] In 1876, after ten years of a stable job in a sober government office, Bram Stoker was promoted to Inspector of Petty Session, a promotion which involved travelling throughout the Irish countryside. These travels led to the writing of his first book, *The Duties of Clerks of Petty Sessions* (1879). It was far from a bestseller and reviewed by Stoker himself as being 'dry-as-dust'.[112]

If Stoker had maintained this career path, as his father would have wanted, he no doubt would have written a sequel to *The Duties of Clerks of Petty Sessions*. Thankfully, he moved to London and eventually wrote *Dracula*. However, these travels through the Irish countryside did eventually find their way into his fiction. The experiences provided the backdrop for his first novel, *The Snake's Pass* (1890), a quaint gothic romance, similar in tone to Emily Brontë's *Wuthering Heights* (1847). Stoker's travels resulted in his assimilation of local legend and colour, which also contributed to his habit of phonetically spelling regional accents. While not exactly a boring novel, if lengthy descriptions on how to drain a bog sound interesting, then this is the book for you.

The original, strategically located castle was completed in 1230. Over the centuries it has been replaced by a loose collection of buildings, most of which date from the mid-eighteenth century to the present, making 'castle' something of a misnomer. During the British occupation of Ireland, Dublin Castle became the vice-regal seat of the occupying government, and the fashionable centre of Anglo-Protestant social life. This was the Dublin Castle of the Stokers' time.

Today, Dublin Castle houses a few state offices, but it lost most of its governmental significance after the Civil War. An entire day can be spent exploring Dublin Castle and its assorted tours and museums. Of particular interest to the macabre-minded may be the Crypt Arts Centre. The theatre itself is located in the crypt of the Chapel Royal, providing a unique atmosphere in which to see a play – amongst once-occupied alcoves. Audiences always give a short gasp of entombed despair when the house lights go down.

Also worth mentioning is the Zozimus Experience, a spellbinding hybrid between ghost tour and street theatre. The tour meets at the Dublin Castle gates, where, at the appropriate hour, tourists are collected by the modern day incarnation of Zozimus, Dublin City's great eccentric-*cum*-tour guide.

On the southern grounds of Dublin Castle stands the Chester Beatty Library, which, along with rotating exhibitions, has a permanent display of sacred texts, illuminated manuscripts and miniature paintings from various world religions. The Chester Beatty Library exhibitions are as essential to visit as the Old Library in Trinity College, where the *Book of Kells* is housed. Bibliophiles take note.

The side lawn of the Chester Beatty Library is the serene Dubhlinn Garden. The garden is on top of what was once a 'black pool' reservoir supplied by the now subterranean Poddle River.[113] '*Dubh linn*' is Irish for 'black pool' hence the origin of both the garden's and the city's name. On top of the garden is a brick snake wrapped around itself in a Celtic design. The black pool and the snake effigy echo the drained bog and defeated Snake King of *The Snake's Pass*, the novel that was the result of Stoker's term as a civil servant in Dublin Castle and his travels in the west of Ireland.

DUBLIN EVENING MAIL

If Abraham Stoker passed one trait on to Bram, it was his fondness for theatre. He often took Bram to Dublin's various theatres to see the great plays. Bram's love for theatre, combined with the tedium of his job at Dublin Castle, resulted in his approaching Henry Maunsell, proprietor and editor of the Protestant newspaper the *Dublin Evening Mail*. The *Mail* was once co-owned by Joseph Sheridan Le Fanu, though not at the time Stoker worked there. And while Le Fanu sold his share of the newspaper around 1869, a couple of years before Stoker's employment, it is still conceivable, even if fanciful, that the two great writers bumped into each other at the *Mail*'s offices.

The former offices of the
Dublin Evening Mail,
38-40 Parliament Street

A clerk by day, Bram pursued his true passion for theatre by the glow of the limelight as an unpaid drama critic from 1871 to 1878. This was the first sign of a real direction in Bram's heretofore shiftless life. As a drama critic, Bram would eventually cross paths with the famous actor Henry Irving, who would later play a significant role in the young journalist's fortunes.

The offices of the *Dublin Evening Mail* were housed in what is now an Italian restaurant on the ground floor and personal injury solicitors on the first. Parliament Street is still cobblestone and the area probably looks much as it did when Bram trudged to the *Dublin Evening Mail*'s offices to write a review after a long night at the theatre.

How to Get There

The sprawling collection of buildings formally known as Dublin Castle is on Dame Street, directly west of Trinity College's main gates. The Crypts Arts Centre (+353 1 671 3387) is in the vaults under the Chapel Royal, and the Zozimus Experience (+353 1 661 8646) meets at the castle gates. Advance booking is essential.

The building that formerly housed the *Dublin Evening Mail* is on the corner of Parliament Street and Dame Street, across the road from Dublin Castle.

SAINT STEPHEN'S GREEN NEIGHBOURHOOD

SAINT STEPHEN'S GREEN NORTH

Stoker moved to 7 Saint Stephen's Green North in 1877.[114] Before he moved here, Stoker had been living at his brother Thornley's house on Harcourt Street. The owner of Stoker's now non-extant address on the Green was a grocer and wine merchant named Robert Smyth. Mr Smyth's shop occupied the ground floor of number 7. Stoker's intention to move to London was quite strong by this point as he wrote, 'London in view!' in a 22 November 1877 diary entry.[115] The ambition to move to London took centre stage in his life.

Bram's former flat on Saint Stephen's Green has now been demolished. The neighbouring 8 Saint Stephen's Green still stands, and up until 2002 housed the same organisation that it did in Bram's time: the Hibernian United Service Club. The Hibernian United Service Club was established in 1832 and, like the Kildare Street Club, was a businessman's club. A Georgian building, like many of Dublin's other fine structures, the Hibernian Club is a reminder of the buildings that once stood on the square's north side.

The same year that Bram had lodgings on Saint Stephen's Green North, Sir Arthur Guinness (Lord Ardilaun) gave to Dublin what is known as the Guinness family's second greatest gift: Saint Stephen's Green Park. The park was originally the site of public punishments including ghastly tortures such as burnings, floggings and hangings. The Green eventually became the semi-private, twenty-two acre front garden of the Iveagh House on Saint Stephen's Green South, also owned by the Guinness family. Saint Stephen's Green is now one of Dublin's

Saint Stephen's Green

most popular tourist attractions and, given its dark past, one of the most sinister. (For more on Saint Stephen's Green, see page 19.)

GAIETY THEATRE

The Gaiety Theatre, or the 'Old Dame' as she is affectionately known, is where Stoker attended Oliver Goldsmith's *She Stoops to Conquer* on 27 November 1871. This was not only the opening night for both the production and the theatre, but would be Stoker's first review for the *Dublin Evening Mail*, marking his first step into the world of the theatre. He was no longer merely an observer. Sensing his son's restlessness, Abraham Stoker gave this final piece of fatherly advice before he died in 1876:

> I am sure you will not think that I want to dictate to you as to the class of acquaintances which you ought to make, but I may offer you some experience of my own early life, which was very varied, and during which I was acquainted with both actors and actresses. Although I am ready to admit that in many instances their society was very agreeable, still I don't think they are altogether desirable acquaintances to those not connected with their own profession (if I may call it,) because it may involve expense and other matters which are not at all times advantageous. Under all the circumstances I believe such acquaintanceship is better avoided.[116]

The Gaiety Theatre is now one of the oldest surviving theatres in Dublin, the others having been demolished over the years. The theatre's distinctive glass awning lends it an unmistakable Venetian air. The interior is furnished with dark wood, and feels stately and old-fashioned. The general effect instantly transports the audience back to 27 November 1871, opening night, alongside the youthful and ambitious Bram.

Gaiety Theatre

ROYAL COLLEGE OF SURGEONS

'What Sutherland?' I asked. Adding that I had been to school with a Dick Sutherland, who had, I believed, gone to the Irish College of Science.'

'Perhaps it's the same gentleman, sir. This is Mr. Richard Sutherland, and I've heerd him say that he was at Stephen's Green.'

— from *The Snake's Pass* (1890)

Standing prominently on Saint Stephen's Green West is the Royal College of Surgeons, founded in 1784, with the current building dating to 1810. Medicine was practically a Stoker family tradition. Two of Stoker's uncles were prominent Dublin physicians and his sister Margaret married another. Of his four brothers, both Richard and George attended the Royal College of Surgeons, while Thornley became the college's president in later life. The fourth brother, Tom, entered the international civil service in India.

Stoker's working notes for *Dracula* show that he contacted a surgeon to accurately describe blood transfusions and autopsies. It has been posited that this surgeon may have been none other than Thornley, Bram's closest brother.[117] The cadaverous connections with the college do not stop there. The building occupies the site of a former Quaker cemetery, and, being a surgeons' college, was also the destination of countless disinterred corpses, care of the Resurrectionists.

Resurrectionists, also known as 'sack'em-ups' were in the unscrupulous and lucrative, not to mention illegal, occupation of providing corpses to local medical schools. Since grave robbers, under the cover of night, were known to

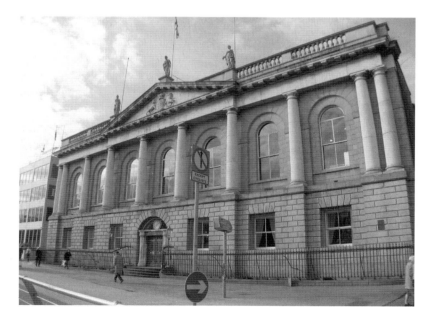

Royal College of Surgeons

escort recently unearthed bodies through the streets of Dublin to the back doors of the medical schools, it was quite common for cemeteries to be guarded. One deterrent was watchtowers. Five such watchtowers can still be seen on the borders of Glasnevin Cemetery on Dublin's north side. The profession of bodysnatching died out when the Anatomy Act was passed in 1832.

For the historically-minded, the Royal College of Surgeons, like the General Post Office on O'Connell Street, became a stronghold during the Easter Rising of 1916. It was from the college that Countess Constance Markievicz commanded a faction of James Connolly's Citizen Army. Like the General Post Office, the stony exterior of the college is still pocked with bullet holes from the fighting. A bust of Countess Markievicz can now be found across the street in Saint Stephen's Green.

CLONMEL HOUSE

[S]he thought it must have been a hundred years or more – the abode of a judge who was held in great terror on account of his harsh sentences and his hostility to prisoners at Assizes. As to what there was against the house itself she could not tell...but there was a general feeling that there was something.

– from 'The Judge's House' (1891)

Just south of Saint Stephen's Green West is the picturesque Harcourt Street, which, despite the progression of time and the recent introduction of a light rail train, still manages to retain the previous centuries within its bricks. Throughout his time in Dublin, Stoker continually gravitated back to Thornley's lodgings on Harcourt Street. In 1870, the entire Stoker family moved into 43 Harcourt Street, which stood on the corner of Harcourt and Charlotte Way.[118] Unfortunately, this end of Harcourt Street has been razed, only to be replaced by a monstrous commercial property that dwarfs the old railway station opposite.

In 1874, two years after Stoker moved to 30 Kildare Street and the rest of the family left for the Continent, Bram's brother Thornley moved to 16 Harcourt Street – Clonmel House. Stoker lodged with Thornley in Clonmel House from late 1874 to mid-1875, and then again in late 1876.[119]

Clonmel House was once the home of John Scott, Lord Clonmel (1739-1798), also known as 'Copper-faced Jack', one of Dublin's most notorious hanging judges. 'In 1792 he hanged a father and son for a minor theft. The son had actually committed the theft but 'Copper-faced Jack' held the father responsible as well.'[120] Could Copper-faced Jack's ghost have haunted Stoker's rooms in Clonmel House? Some Stoker researchers assert that his stay at Clonmel House may have influenced his traditional, and certainly effective, ghost story 'The Judge's House' (1891).[121]

The story follows an unfortunate college student named Malcolmson, who, in search of a quiet place to study, rents a decaying house in a small village. The superstitious villagers, as superstitious villagers are wont to

Clonmel House

do, warn Malcolmson that the ghost of a hanging judge haunts the house. The mathematically-minded Malcolmson, as most rationalists are wont to do, ignores the warning.

Much to Malcolmson's dismay, things go bump in the night and he is plagued by a growing number of ever more dauntless rats. Stoker had a knack for using rats to create a mounting atmosphere of horror as they feature in *Dracula*, his short story 'Burial of the Rats' (1891), and 'The Judge's House':

> To-night the rats disturbed him more than they had done on the previous night. How they scampered up and down and under and over! How they squeaked, and scratched, and gnawed! How they, getting bolder by degrees, came to the mouths of their holes and to the chinks and cracks and crannies in the wainscoting till their eyes shone like tiny lamps as the firelight rose and fell.[122]

Before long, the spectral judge, as fiendish as the real-life Copper-faced Jack, reveals himself to Malcolmson, the rare student in search of peace and quiet:

> At the sound the Judge, who had been keeping his eyes fixed on Malcolmson, looked up, and a scowl of diabolical anger overspread his face. His eyes fairly glowed like hot coals, and he stamped his foot with a sound that seemed to make the house shake... Malcolmson stood rigid as a corpse. He felt the Judge's icy fingers touch his throat as he adjusted the rope. The noose tightened – tightened.[123]

Poor Malcolmson would have been better off at the pub. Fortunately for us, Copper-Face Jack's Nightclub is only a few doors away from Clonmel House. Today Clonmel House is home to the non-spectral Finnish Embassy and

The Iveagh Gardens

Saagar Indian Cuisine, a restaurant that serves the best Indian food in town, complimented by impeccable service.

George Bernard Shaw also lived for a short while on Harcourt Street. His home at number 60 is now the Harcourt Hotel. The paths of Stoker and Shaw later crossed on London's theatre circuit. Shaw, as a theatre critic, seemed to have it in for Henry Irving, Stoker's employer in London, and once referred to Stoker himself as Irving's 'henchman'.[124]

Number 4 Harcourt Street, a few doors north of Clonmel House, was the birthplace of Lord Edward Carson (1854-1935). Carson was the barrister in the famous 'gross indecency' trial that eventually sent fellow Dubliner Oscar Wilde on his way to Reading Gaol in 1895.

Once the front garden of Clonmel House, the Iveagh Gardens are now the extraordinary back garden of the Iveagh House on Saint Stephen's Green. Benjamin Lee Guinness bought the gardens in 1863 and had them landscaped to their present design. One of the best-kept secrets in the entire city of Dublin, the gardens remain mostly vacant on the hottest days of summer, even when Saint Stephen's Green is brimming with tourists. One entrance is a small doorway in a wall behind the National Concert Hall. The other is a hidden gate at the end of Clonmel Street, near Clonmel House. In 2005, another entrance was opened on the park's south side from Hatch Street Upper. With any luck, this third entrance will also be overlooked by the masses.

The isolated gardens give one the feeling that somewhere in the overgrowth lie the stoic remains of a ruined manor. With chipped and weathered statues throughout, the gardens resemble something out of Henry James's *The Turn of the Screw* (1898). The park's dark laneways and ivy-covered walls balance out the sunlit lawns and sparkling fountains. Also of note are the Victorian rosarium and a tiny hedge maze, at the centre of which stands a solitary sundial. You can pause for a moment's rest near the park's beautiful, artificial grotto before moving on.

With Saint Stephen's Green often overcrowded, and the Iveagh Gardens less than two blocks away, it is a wonder that the park is so often overlooked. Perhaps there's more in the garden's dark and desolate corners than meets the eye.

ELY HOUSE

[A]nd me, with my poor wife dead to me, but alive by Church's law, though no wits, all gone – even I who am faithful a husband to this now-no-wife.

– from *Dracula* (1897)

Long after Stoker moved to London, Thornley moved with his wife Emily to 8 Ely Place, known as Ely House. Ely House, which proudly overlooks Saint Stephen's Green from the end of Hume Street, was originally built for the Earl of Ely.

Oddly enough, John Fitzgibbon, the Earl of Clare (1749-1802), who lived at nearby 6 Ely Place, was another notorious hanging judge locally known as 'Black Jack'.[125]

Bram's brother Thornley made a name for himself in the medical field, and became a well-known physician in Dublin and beyond. Queen Victoria knighted Thornley for his contributions to medicine in the same ceremony during which she knighted the actor Henry Irving. Sir Thornley lived in Ely House until his wife died in 1910, after which he moved south to Hatch Street, where he spent the rest of his life.

Writer and statesman Oliver St John Gogarty also lived on Ely Place, and wrote of Sir Thornley's opulence:

Ely House
overlooking Hume Street

T]he house is filled with period furniture, of which [Thornley] is a collector and connoisseur. Chippendale Adams and old silver candelabra match the silver jambs of the doors, and are contemporary with the silver linings of the great fireplace, under their mantels of Sienna and statuary marble.[126]

Gogarty also relates novelist George Moore's comments on Sir Thornley's lavish furnishings:

Moore went over to his empty chair, balanced it on its hind legs, admired what Sir Thornley would call 'the excellent skin' of its glossy Chippendale wood, and turning from his scrutiny, with a look of inquiry towards his host, asked: 'A cancer, Sir Thornley, or a gallstone?' referring to Sir Thornley's habit of buying after a big operation 'a museum piece.' [127]

During one of Sir Thornley's dinner parties, a nude Lady Emily, who was suffering from dementia, burst into the party and yelled, 'I like a little intelligent conversation!' Mortified, Sir Thornley asked his guests to keep quiet about the incident. A full account of the incident can now be read in Oliver St John Gogarty's autobiography, *As I Was Going Down Sackville Street* (1937).[128]

Also of interest is 4 Ely Place, the former home of George Moore, who attended the aforementioned party with fellow Sir Thornley critic, Gogarty. Next door is 3 Ely Place, known in 1891 as 'the Lodge'. The Lodge was the meeting house for the Dublin chapter of the fashionable Theosophical Society founded by Madame Helena Blavatsky in 1875. Among the society's members who had rooms at the Lodge were George William Russell (Æ) and his companion and fellow poet William Butler Yeats when the latter was going through his Gnostic, Enochian and Rosicrucian phases.

THE HUGUENOT CEMETERY

There, in the full glare of the light, the whole material and sordid side of death seemed startlingly real.

– from *The Jewel of Seven Stars* (1903)

Considering the location of this cemetery, no quote could be truer. Although unrelated to Stoker, one must wonder how many oblivious Dubliners walk by this *memento mori* every day? The beautifully restored cemetery seems an anachronistic anomaly on the somewhat modern and lively stretch of Saint Stephen's Green North and Merrion Row. The city's macabre leanings often hide in broad daylight. The plaque affixed to the gate explains the cemetery's history:

Huguenot Cemetery founded in 1693 by the French Huguenot non-conformist churches of Dublin, and now belonging to the French Huguenot Fund restored in 1988 through a grant from the French Ministry of Foreign Affairs in association with FÁS.

It may be surprising to learn that an estimated 600 people are buried in the tiny cemetery, though given its lengthy usage, this may not be so absurd. The most recent burial was in 1901 while the first was in 1693, making this the oldest Huguenot non-conformist cemetery in Europe.[129]

It may be worth pointing out that the two other writers addressed in this book, Charles Maturin and Joseph Sheridan Le Fanu, are of French Huguenot descent. Bram was a Protestant.

Unfortunately, the tiny park is closed to the public, forcing visitors to peer through the iron gates at the charnel yard beyond.

THE SHELBOURNE HOTEL

Soul had looked into soul. From that hour began a friendship as profound, as close, as lasting, as can be between two men.

– from *Personal Reminiscences of Henry Irving* (1906)

Stoker lost both his surrogate father and birth father in 1876 when Sir William Wilde died on 19 April followed by Abraham Stoker on 10 October in La Cava, Italy.[130] But he would not be without a father figure for long. In December of the same year, Stoker saw an actor he had long admired perform in *Hamlet* – Henry Irving. Stoker wrote a favourable, yet balanced review of this performance in the *Dublin Evening Mail*. Impressed by the journalist's even-handed observations, Irving invited the twenty-nine year old to dinner that night.

Henry Irving and Bram Stoker first met in Dublin's luxurious Shelbourne Hotel. After dinner, the evening continued with cigars and port whilst Irving recited Thomas Hood's poem 'The Dream of Eugene Aram'. The impromptu performance left Stoker absolutely mesmerised. Irving and Stoker became close friends, and over the next two years, whenever Irving toured Ireland, the two were often found in each other's company.

The Shelbourne Hotel

Finally, in 1878, Irving asked Stoker to move to London and manage his new business endeavour, the historic Lyceum Theatre. Stoker accepted and, after a rushed marriage to Florence Balcombe, the couple moved to England. His wish to move to London was fulfilled, and his love for the theatre must have made the offer a dream incarnate.

Stoker did not know it, but at that meeting on a cold December night in 1876, he came face to face with Count Dracula.[131] Stoker would later put his heart and soul into running the Lyceum Theatre, often times neglecting his personal life. Henry Irving, an invaluable friend and a domineering employer, had Stoker in his thrall, for better or for worse. It was Stoker's energy that sustained the Lyceum, making it the most celebrated theatre of its day. When the Lyceum closed, Stoker, as if drained of his life-blood by the Count himself, became a forlorn waif, as aimless at the end of his life as he was at the beginning.

The Shelbourne Hotel has been a strong presence on the north side of Saint Stephen's Green since it opened its doors. Originally a collection of three Georgian homes, the buildings were converted to a hotel by Martin Burke in 1824. Along with the Merrion around the corner, the Shelbourne is considered Dublin's most fashionable hotel. The building's most notable features are the torch-bearing Egyptian women who eternally guard and illuminate the front entrance. The fanciful may find a passing resemblance to Queen Tera from Stoker's *The Jewel of Seven Stars*. Like most historical buildings in Dublin, the Shelbourne Hotel has connections with the beginning of Irish nationhood. One could even say that Ireland was born in the Shelbourne as the *Constitution of the Irish Free State* was drafted here in 1922.

While rooms in the hotel may be a bit pricey for the thrifty tourist, there is always the Shelbourne Bar, to give visitors a taste of the hotel's extravagance. And they don't pull a bad pint either. *Sláinte!*

The Shelbourne's torch-bearer

How to Get There

All the locations around Saint Stephen's Green are best visited in an anti-clockwise rotation, starting at the top of Grafton Street with 7 Saint Stephen's Green North.

The Gaiety Theatre (+353 1 677 1717) is located on South King Street, and can be easily seen from the top of Grafton Street. Also within a short walking distance is the Royal College of Surgeons (+353 1 402 2100), the dominant building on Saint Stephen's Green West.

From the Royal College of Surgeons, continue south to where Harcourt Street meets Saint Stephen's Green's south-west corner. A short distance down Harcourt Street, on the right hand side, is Clonmel House. In the basement of Clonmel House is Saagar Indian Cuisine (+353 1 475 5012). Just across the road is Clonmel Street, at the end of which is the inconspicuous entrance to the Iveagh Gardens.

While walking east on Saint Stephen's Green's southern border, take care to notice the Iveagh House, formerly owned by the Guinness family; and the Newman House (+353 1 706 7422), the college where poet Gerard Manly Hopkins (1844-1889) lectured and James Joyce (1882-1941) attended, though not at the same time. The Newman House also has a worthwhile tour.

From Saint Stephen's Green East, take a right on Hume Street. Ely House is on Ely Place overlooking Hume Street. From Ely Place to the Huguenot cemetery, continue north along Ely Place and take a left onto Merrion Row. This leads directly back to Saint Stephen's Green North. Along this stretch are the Huguenot cemetery and the Shelbourne Hotel (+353 1 663 4500).

Saint Michan's Church

Saint Michan's is one of Dublin's oldest Christian churches and dates back to 1095. For centuries before that, as is often the case with European churches, the site was used for pagan worship. The current building, most of which dates from 1685, is thought to be the oldest building on the north side of the city, and was for a number of years the only church on the north side. Saint Michan's striking Gothic tower still commands attention on Dublin's ever-changing skyline, standing with defiant prominence behind the imposing dome of the Four Courts, built one hundred years later.

The church's interior, seemingly Spartan in decoration, yields a treasury of ornamental detail for those with the patience to stop and look. Of the more notable features is an organ, which tradition holds was used by Handel when he debuted *The Messiah* at Neal's Music Hall on Fishamble Street in 1742.[132] The keyboard of the original organ has been replaced, but the old keyboard, graced by Handel's inspired fingertips, is on display at the rear of the chapel. There is also an elaborate carving dating from 1724. The carving boasts seventeen realistic-looking musical instruments carved with intricate precision from a single piece of wood.

The church does have a connection to Stoker, which can be found in Saint Michan's world-famous vaults.

Saint Michan's Church

The vault's quartet
of mummies
(courtesy of Saint
Michan's Church)

SAINT MICHAN'S VAULTS

> You may put a mummy in a glass case and hermetically seal it so that no corroding
> air can get within; but all the same it will exhale its odour. One might think that
> four or five thousand years would exhaust the olfactory qualities of anything; but
> experience teaches us that these smells remain, and that their secrets are unknown
> to us. Today they are as much mysteries as they were when the embalmers put the
> body in a bath of natron...
>
>   – from *The Jewel of Seven Stars* (1903)

After buying a ticket in the church's reception, you will enter the vaults from the
church's south side, down rough-hewn steps into the cool and dry vaults below.
Like the popular images of Dracula's Castle, everything is covered with the dust
of the centuries, cobwebs hanging cinematically from the ceiling. The church
above dates back to a reconstruction in 1685, but the vaults below date back to
the original church built in 1095.

The vault's most famous attraction is a quartet of mummies at the far end of
the passage who have been on display for over one hundred years. The oldest
mummy is reputed to be an 800-year-old knight who fought in the Crusades. It
is tradition for visitors to the vaults to 'shake hands with the Crusader' for good
luck. While this is discouraged today due to the brittleness of the Crusader's
hand and wrist, visitors are still encouraged to touch his finger. This is also
presumably for good luck, not just morbid curiosity.

It is conceivable that Stoker, who had an affinity for the macabre, visited
these mummies. It is sometimes said that these mummies influenced his novel
of a mummy's revenge, *The Jewel of Seven Stars*. Certainly, the mummified

cadavers' creepiness permeates up through the ages to chill even the most insensitive of souls.

Another more substantial connection to Bram is that a branch of the Stoker family has a vault somewhere under the church, though it is unclear which of the church's many sealed vaults is theirs. Some scholars claim that Stoker's mum Charlotte is buried here, but her remains are almost certainly resting, un-mummified, on the city's south side.[133] The likelihood that Stoker visited the vaults at some point during his time in Dublin is quite high, and with a family vault on the premises, he certainly had a reason.

How to Get There

Saint Michan's Church is on Church Street on Dublin's north side. To get there from O'Connell Bridge, walk west along the north side of the Liffey. Church Street intersects with Arran Quay and Inns Quay just past the unmistakable Four Courts. As a regular Dublin tourist attraction, there are several signs pointing the way.

EPILOGUE

At the end of 1878, Stoker and his new wife left Ireland behind. They settled in central London where Stoker took the position as manager of Henry Irving's Lyceum until the theatre closed its doors in 1902. During that time the Lyceum became the jewel of London's theatre world, and Stoker continued to lead a most fascinating life. After the theatre closed its door, Stoker continued working as Sir Henry's touring manager. The company went on six tours of America and were planning a seventh when Irving passed away in 1905. As a manager, Stoker spent so much time with the theatre that it is a wonder he found time to write the eighteen books that were eventually published under his name, starting with *Duties of a Petty Clerk* in 1879 and finishing with the posthumous collection of short stories *Dracula's Guest and Others Weird Stories,* published in 1914.

Nearly all of Stoker's novels and stories have been forgotten by the general reading public – save for one. From a ghastly germ sown in the spring of 1890, Stoker began work on a book that would rank among royalty in the kingdom of horror literature. Originally entitled *The Un-Dead*, Stoker's seminal vampire novel *Dracula* was published seven years later to general indifference. It was not until 'its successful run as a Broadway play in the late 1920s and its subsequent conversion into the Universal Studios hit movie *Dracula* (1931)' that Count Dracula managed to mesmerise the masses.[134] After all, who can vanquish from their mind the iconic and undying images of Bela Lugosi or Christopher Lee as the infamous Count?

After Irving passed away in 1905, having no stable source of income, Stoker turned to full-time writing. Save for *The Lair of the White Worm*'s small cult following, due in part to the Ken Russell film of the same title, Stoker would write no other work that came close to rivalling the popularity of *Dracula*. On 20 April 1912, Bram Stoker passed away at his home in London. It has often been rumoured that he died of syphilis, but this is merely speculation.[135] His death certificate reads, 'Locomotor Ataxy 6 Months, Granular Contracted Kidney. Exhaustion.' Stoker was cremated and his ashes were deposited in a stone urn in Golders Green Crematorium, London, where his only son Irving Noel Thornley Stoker joined him in 1961.

Bram Stoker's life and fiction came to fruition in England. London was where Stoker found success in the theatre business and continued to write but the roots of his life and imagination were planted firmly in Dublin. Bram Stoker, until his thirty-first year, took his nourishment from the lifeblood of Ireland, from its folktales and stories. The very soul of Dublin was absorbed by the man who would later, like his protagonist Jonathan Harker, deliver Count Dracula to the world.

THE JUDGE'S HOUSE

by Bram Stoker

When the time for his examination drew near Malcolm Malcolmson made up his mind to go somewhere to read by himself. He feared the attractions of the seaside, and also he feared completely rural isolation, for of old he knew its charms, and so he determined to find some unpretentious little town where there would be nothing to distract him. He refrained from asking suggestions from any of his friends, for he argued that each would recommend some place of which he had knowledge, and where he had already acquaintances. As Malcolmson wished to avoid friends he had no wish to encumber himself with the attention or friends' friends, and so he determined to look out for a place for himself. He packed a portmanteau with some clothes and all the books he required, and then took ticket for the first name on the local time-table which he did not know.

When at the end of three hours' journey he alighted at Benchurch, he felt satisfied that he had so far obliterated his tracks as to be sure of having a peaceful opportunity of pursuing his studies. He went straight to the one inn which the sleepy little place contained, and put up for the night. Benchurch was a market town, and once in three weeks was crowded to excess, but for the remainder of the twenty-one days it was as attractive as a desert. Malcolmson looked around the day after his arrival to try to find quarters more isolated than even so quiet an inn as 'The Good Traveller' afforded. There was only one place which took his fancy, and it certainly satisfied his wildest ideas regarding quiet; in fact, quiet was not the proper word to apply to it – desolation was the only term conveying any suitable idea of its isolation. It was an old rambling, heavy-built house of the Jacobean style, with heavy gables and windows, unusually small, and set higher than was customary in such houses, and was surrounded with a high brick wall massively built. Indeed, on examination, it looked more like a fortified house than an ordinary dwelling. But all these things pleased Malcolmson. 'Here,' he thought, 'is the very spot I have been looking for, and if I can only get opportunity of using it I shall be happy.' His joy was increased when he realised beyond doubt that it was not at present inhabited.

From the post-office he got the name of the agent, who was rarely surprised at the application to rent a part of the old house. Mr Carnford, the local lawyer and agent, was a genial old gentleman, and frankly confessed his delight at anyone being willing to live in the house.

'To tell you the truth,' said he, 'I should be only too happy, on behalf of the owners, to let anyone have the house rent free for a term of years if only to accustom the people here to see it inhabited. It has been so long empty that some kind of absurd prejudice has grown up about it, and this can be best put down by its occupation – if only,' he added with a sly glance at Malcolmson, 'by a scholar like yourself, who wants it quiet for a time.'

Malcolmson thought it needless to ask the agent about the 'absurd prejudice'; he knew he would get more information, if he should require it, on that subject from other quarters. He paid his three months' rent, got a receipt, and the name of an old woman who would probably undertake to 'do' for him, and came away with the keys in his pocket. He then went to the landlady of the inn, who was a cheerful and most kindly person, and asked her advice as to such stores and provisions as he would be likely to require. She threw up her hands in amazement when he told her where he was going to settle himself.

'Not in the Judge's House!' she said, and grew pale as she spoke. He explained the locality of the house, saying that he did not know its name. When he had finished she answered:

'Aye, sure enough – sure enough the very place! It is the Judge's House sure enough.' He asked her to tell him about the place, why so called, and what there was against it. She told him that it was so called locally because it had been many years before – how long she could not say, as she was herself from another part of the country, but she thought it must have been a hundred years or more – the abode of a judge who was held in great terror on account of his harsh sentences and his hostility to prisoners at Assizes. As to what there was against the house itself she could not tell. She had often asked, but no one could inform her; but there was a general feeling that there was *something,* and for her own part she would not take all the money in Drinkwater's Bank and stay in the house an hour by herself. Then she apologised to Malcolmson for her disturbing talk.

'It is too bad of me, sir, and you – and a young gentleman, too – if you will pardon me saying it, going to live there all alone. If you were my boy – and you'll excuse me for saying it – you wouldn't sleep there a night, not if I had to go there myself and pull the big alarm bell that's on the roof!' The good creature was so manifestly in earnest, and was so kindly in her intentions, that Malcolmson, although amused, was touched. He told her kindly how much he appreciated her interest in him, and added:

'But, my dear Mrs Witham, indeed you need not be concerned about me! A man who is reading for the Mathematical Tripos has too much to think of to be disturbed by any of these mysterious "somethings," and his work is of too exact and prosaic a kind to allow of his having any corner in his mind for mysteries of any kind. Harmonical Progression, Permutations and Combinations, and Elliptic Functions have sufficient mysteries for me!' Mrs. Witham kindly undertook to see after his commissions, and he went himself to look for the old woman who had been recommended to him. When he returned to the Judge's House with her, after an interval of a couple of hours, he found Mrs Witham herself waiting with several men and boys carrying parcels, and an upholsterer's man with a bed in a cart, for she said, though tables and chairs might be all very well, a bed that hadn't been aired for mayhap fifty years was not proper for young bones to lie on. She was evidently curious to see the inside of the house; and though manifestly so afraid of the 'somethings' that at the slightest sound she clutched on to Malcolmson, whom she never left for a moment, went over the whole place.

After his examination of the house, Malcolmson decided to take up his abode in the great dining-room, which was big enough to serve for all his requirements; and Mrs Witham, with the aid of the charwoman, Mrs Dempster, proceeded to arrange matters. When the hampers were brought in and unpacked, Malcolmson saw that with much kind forethought she had sent from her own kitchen sufficient provisions to last for a few days. Before going she expressed all sorts of kind wishes; and at the door turned and said:

'And perhaps, sir, as the room is big and draughty it might be well to have one of those big screens put round your bed at night – though, truth to tell, I would die myself if I were to be so shut in with all kinds of – of "things," that put their heads round the sides, or over the top, and look on me!' The image which she had called up was too much for her nerves, and she fled incontinently.

Mrs Dempster sniffed in a superior manner as the landlady disappeared, and remarked that for her own part she wasn't afraid of all the bogies in the kingdom.

'I'll tell you what it is, sir,' she said; 'bogies is all kinds and sorts of things – except bogies! Rats and mice, and beetles; and creaky doors, and loose slates, and broken panes, and stiff drawer handles, that stay out when you pull them and then fall down in the middle of the night. Look at the wainscot of the room! It is old – hundreds of years old! Do you think there's no rats and beetles there! And do you imagine, sir, that you won't see none of them! Rats is bogies, I tell you, and bogies is rats; and don't you get to think anything else!'

'Mrs Dempster,' said Malcolmson gravely, making her a polite bow, 'you know more than a Senior Wrangler! And let me say, that, as a mark of esteem for your indubitable soundness of head and heart, I shall, when I go, give you possession of this house, and let you stay here by yourself for the last two months of my tenancy, for four weeks will serve my purpose.'

'Thank you kindly, sir!' she answered, 'but I couldn't sleep away from home a night. I am in Greenhow's Charity, and if I slept a night away from my rooms I should lose all I have got to live on. The rules is very strict; and there's too many watching for a vacancy for me to run any risks in the matter. Only for that, sir, I'd gladly come here and attend on you altogether during your stay.'

'My good woman,' said Malcolmson hastily, 'I have come here on purpose to obtain solitude; and believe me that I am grateful to the late Greenhow for having so organised his admirable charity – whatever it is – that I am perforce denied the opportunity of suffering from such a form of temptation! Saint Anthony himself could not be more rigid on the point!'

The old woman laughed harshly. 'Ah, you young gentlemen,' she said, 'you don't fear for naught; and belike you'll get all the solitude you want here.' She set to work with her cleaning; and by nightfall, when Malcolmson returned from his walk – he always had one of his books to study as he walked – he found the room swept and tidied, a fire burning in the old hearth, the lamp lit, and the table spread for supper with Mrs Witham's excellent fare. 'This is comfort, indeed,' he said, as he rubbed his hands.

When he had finished his supper, and lifted the tray to the other end of the great oak dining-table, he got out his books again, put fresh wood on the fire, trimmed his lamp, and set himself down to a spell of real hard work. He went on without pause till about eleven o'clock, when he knocked off for a bit to fix his fire and lamp, and to make himself a cup of tea. He had always been a tea-drinker, and during his college life had sat late at work and had taken tea late. The rest was a great luxury to him, and he enjoyed it with a sense of delicious, voluptuous ease. The renewed fire leaped and sparkled, and threw quaint shadows through the great old room; and as he sipped his hot tea he revelled in the sense of isolation from his kind. Then it was that he began to notice for the first time what a noise the rats were making.

'Surely,' he thought, 'they cannot have been at it all the time I was reading. Had they been, I must have noticed it!' Presently, when the noise increased, he satisfied himself that it was really new. It was evident that at first the rats had been frightened at the presence of a stranger, and the light of fire and lamp; but that as the time went on they had grown bolder and were now disporting themselves as was their wont.

How busy they were! And hark to the strange noises! Up and down behind the old wainscot, over the ceiling and under the floor they raced, and gnawed, and scratched! Malcolmson smiled to himself as he recalled to mind the saying of Mrs Dempster, 'Bogies is rats, and rats is bogies!' The tea began to have its effect of intellectual and nervous stimulus, he saw with joy another long spell of work to be done before the night was past, and in the sense of security which it gave him, he allowed himself the luxury of a good look round the room. He took his lamp in one hand, and went all around, wondering that so quaint and beautiful an old house had been so long neglected. The carving of the oak on the panels of the wainscot was fine, and on and round the doors and windows it was beautiful and of rare merit. There were some old pictures on the walls, but they were coated so thick with dust and dirt that he could not distinguish any detail of them, though he held his lamp as high as he could over his head. Here and there as he went round he saw some crack or hole blocked for a moment by the face of a rat with its bright eyes glittering in the light, but in an instant it was gone, and a squeak and a scamper followed.

The thing that most struck him, however, was the rope of the great alarm bell on the roof, which hung down in a corner of the room on the right-hand side of the fireplace. He pulled up close to the hearth a great high-backed carved oak chair, and sat down to his last cup of tea. When this was done he made up the fire, and went back to his work, sitting at the corner of the table, having the fire to his left. For a while the rats disturbed him somewhat with their perpetual scampering, but he got accustomed to the noise as one does to the ticking of a clock or to the roar of moving water; and he became so immersed in his work that everything in the world, except the problem which he was trying to solve, passed away from him.

He suddenly looked up, his problem was still unsolved, and there was in the air that sense of the hour before the dawn, which is so dread to doubtful life. The noise of the rats had ceased. Indeed it seemed to him that it must have ceased but lately and that it was the sudden cessation which had disturbed him. The fire had fallen low, but still it threw out a deep red glow. As he looked he started in spite of his *sang froid*.

There on the great high-backed carved oak chair by the right side of the fireplace sat an enormous rat, steadily glaring at him with baleful eyes. He made a motion to it as though to hunt it away, but it did not stir. Then he made the motion of throwing something. Still it did not stir, but showed its great white teeth angrily, and its cruel eyes shone in the lamplight with an added vindictiveness.

Malcolmson felt amazed, and seizing the poker from the hearth ran at it to kill it. Before, however, he could strike it, the rat, with a squeak that sounded like the concentration of hate, jumped upon the floor, and, running up the rope of the alarm bell, disappeared in the darkness beyond the range of the green-shaded lamp. Instantly, strange to say, the noisy scampering of the rats in the wainscot began again.

By this time Malcolmson's mind was quite off the problem; and as a shrill cock-crow outside told him of the approach of morning, he went to bed and to sleep.

He slept so sound that he was not even waked by Mrs Dempster coming in to make up his room. It was only when she had tidied up the place and got his breakfast ready and tapped on the screen which closed in his bed that he woke. He was a little tired still after his night's hard work, but a strong cup of tea soon freshened him up, and, taking his book, he went out for his morning walk, bringing with him a few sandwiches lest he should not care to return till dinner time. He found a quiet walk between high elms some way outside the town, and here he spent the greater part of the day studying his Laplace. On his return he looked in to see Mrs Witham and to thank her for her kindness. When she saw him coming through the diamond-paned bay-window of her sanctum she came out to meet him and asked him in. She looked at him searchingly and shook her head as she said:

'You must not overdo it, sir. You are paler this morning than you should be. Too late hours and too hard work on the brain isn't good for any man! But tell me, sir, how did you pass the night? Well, I hope? But, my heart! Sir, I was glad when Mrs Dempster told me this morning that you were all right and sleeping sound when she went in.'

'Oh, I was all right,' he answered, smiling, 'the "somethings" didn't worry me, as yet. Only the rats; and they had a circus, I tell you, all over the place. There was one wicked looking old devil that sat up on my own chair by the fire, and wouldn't go till I took the poker to him, and then he ran up the rope of the alarm bell and got to somewhere up the wall or the ceiling – I couldn't see where, it was so dark.'

'Mercy on us,' said Mrs Witham, 'an old devil, and sitting on a chair by the fireside! Take care, sir! Take care! There's many a true word spoken in jest.'

'How do you mean? 'Pon my word I don't understand.'

'An old devil! The old devil, perhaps. There! Sir, you needn't laugh,' for Malcolmson had broken into a hearty peal. 'You young folks thinks it easy to laugh at things that makes older ones shudder. Never mind, sir! Never mind!

Please God, you'll laugh all the time. It's what I wish you myself!' and the good lady beamed all over in sympathy with his enjoyment, her fears gone for a moment.

'Oh, forgive me!' said Malcolmson presently. 'Don't think me rude; but the idea was too much for me – that the old devil himself was on the chair last night!' And at the thought he laughed again. Then he went home to dinner.

This evening the scampering of the rats began earlier; indeed it had been going on before his arrival, and only ceased whilst his presence by its freshness disturbed them. After dinner he sat by the fire for a while and had a smoke; and then, having cleared his table, began to work as before. To-night the rats disturbed him more than they had done on the previous night. How they scampered up and down and under and over! How they squeaked, and scratched, and gnawed! How they, getting bolder by degrees, came to the mouths of their holes and to the chinks and cracks and crannies in the wainscoting till their eyes shone like tiny lamps as the firelight rose and fell. But to him, now doubtless accustomed to them, their eyes were not wicked; only their playfulness touched him. Sometimes the boldest of them made sallies out on the floor or along the mouldings of the wainscot. Now and again as they disturbed him Malcolmson made a sound to frighten them, smiting the table with his hand or giving a fierce 'Hsh, hsh,' so that they fled straightway to their holes.

And so the early part of the night wore on; and despite the noise Malcolmson got more and more immersed in his work.

All at once he stopped, as on the previous night, being overcome by a sudden sense of silence. There was not the faintest sound of gnaw, or scratch, or squeak. The silence was as of the grave. He remembered the odd occurrence of the previous night, and instinctively he looked at the chair standing close by the fireside. And then a very odd sensation thrilled through him.

There, on the great old high-backed carved oak chair beside the fireplace sat the same enormous rat, steadily glaring at him with baleful eyes.

Instinctively he took the nearest thing to his hand, a book of logarithms, and flung it at it. The book was badly aimed and the rat did not stir, so again the poker performance of the previous night was repeated; and again the rat, being closely pursued, fled up the rope of the alarm bell. Strangely too, the departure of this rat was instantly followed by the renewal of the noise made by the general rat community. On this occasion, as on the previous one, Malcolmson could not see at what part of the room the rat disappeared, for the green shade of his lamp left the upper part of the room in darkness, and the fire had burned low.

On looking at his watch he found it was close on midnight; and, not sorry for the *divertissement*, he made up his fire and made himself his nightly pot of tea. He had got through a good spell of work, and thought himself entitled to a cigarette; and so he sat on the great carved oak chair before the fire and enjoyed it. Whilst smoking he began to think that he would like to know where the rat disappeared to, for he had certain ideas for the morrow not entirely disconnected with a rat-trap. Accordingly he lit another lamp and placed it so that it would shine well into the right-hand corner of the wall by the fireplace.

'Their eyes shone like tiny lamps as the firelight rose and fell'

Then he got all the books he had with him, and placed them handy to throw at the vermin. Finally he lifted the rope of the alarm bell and placed the end of it on the table, fixing the extreme end under the lamp. As he handled it he could not help noticing how pliable it was, especially for so strong a rope, and one not in use. 'You could hang a man with it,' he thought to himself. When his preparations were made he looked around, and said complacently:

'There now, my friend, I think we shall learn something of you this time!' He began his work again, and though as before somewhat disturbed at first by the noise of the rats, soon lost himself in his propositions and problems.

Again he was called to his immediate surroundings suddenly. This time it might not have been the sudden silence only which took his attention; there was a slight movement of the rope, and the lamp moved. Without stirring, he looked to see if his pile of books was within range, and then cast his eye along the rope. As he looked he saw the great rat drop from the rope on the oak armchair and sit there glaring at him. He raised a book in his right hand, and taking careful aim, flung it at the rat. The latter, with a quick movement, sprang aside and dodged the missile. He then took another book, and a third, and flung them one after another at the rat, but each time unsuccessfully. At last, as he stood with a book poised in his hand to throw, the rat squeaked and seemed afraid. This made Malcolmson more than ever eager to strike, and the book flew and struck the rat a resounding blow. It gave a terrified squeak, and turning on its pursuer a look of terrible malevolence, ran up the chair-back and made a great jump to the rope of the alarm bell and ran up it like lightning. The lamp rocked under the sudden strain, but it was a heavy one and did not topple over. Malcolmson kept his eyes on the rat, and saw it by the light of the second lamp leap to a moulding of the wainscot and disappear through a hole in one of the great pictures which hung on the wall, obscured and invisible through its coating of dirt and dust.

'I shall look up my friend's habitation in the morning,' said the student, as he went over to collect his books. 'The third picture from the fireplace; I shall not forget.' He picked up the books one by one, commenting on them as he lifted them. '*Conic Sections* he does not mind, nor *Cycloidal Oscillations*, nor the *Principia*, nor *Quaternions*, nor *Thermodynamics*. Now for the book that fetched him!' Malcolmson took it up and looked at it. As he did so he started, and a sudden pallor overspread his face. He looked round uneasily and shivered slightly, as he murmured to himself:

'The Bible my mother gave me! What an odd coincidence.' He sat down to work again, and the rats in the wainscot renewed their gambols. They did not disturb him, however; somehow their presence gave him a sense of companionship. But he could not attend to his work, and after striving to master the subject on which he was engaged gave it up in despair, and went to bed as the first streak of dawn stole in through the eastern window.

He slept heavily but uneasily, and dreamed much; and when Mrs Dempster woke him late in the morning he seemed ill at ease, and for a few minutes did not seem to realise exactly where he was. His first request rather surprised the servant.

'Mrs Dempster, when I am out to-day I wish you would get the steps and dust or wash those pictures – specially that one the third from the fireplace – I want to see what they are.'

Late in the afternoon Malcolmson worked at his books in the shaded walk, and the cheerfulness of the previous day came back to him as the day wore on, and he found that his reading was progressing well. He had worked out to a satisfactory conclusion all the problems which had as yet baffled him, and it was in a state of jubilation that he paid a visit to Mrs Witham at 'The Good Traveller.' He found a stranger in the cosy sitting-room with the landlady, who was introduced to him as Dr Thornhill. She was not quite at ease, and this, combined with the Doctor's plunging at once into a series of questions, made Malcolmson come to the conclusion that his presence was not an accident, so without preliminary he said:

'Dr Thornhill, I shall with pleasure answer you any question you may choose to ask me if you will answer me one question first.'

The Doctor seemed surprised, but he smiled and answered at once. 'Done! What is it?'

'Did Mrs Witham ask you to come here and see me and advise me?'

Dr Thornhill for a moment was taken aback, and Mrs Witham got fiery red and turned away; but the Doctor was a frank and ready man, and he answered at once and openly:

'She did: but she didn't intend you to know it. I suppose it was my clumsy haste that made you suspect. She told me that she did not like the idea of your being in that house all by yourself, and that she thought you took too much strong tea. In fact, she wants me to advise you if possible to give up the tea and the very late hours. I was a keen student in my time, so I suppose I may take the liberty of a college man, and without offence, advise you not quite as a stranger.'

Malcolmson with a bright smile held out his hand. 'Shake! As they say in America,' he said. 'I must thank you for your kindness and Mrs Witham too, and your kindness deserves a return on my part. I promise to take no more strong tea – no tea at all till you let me – and I shall go to bed to-night at one o'clock at latest. Will that do?'

'Capital,' said the Doctor. 'Now tell us all that you noticed in the old house,' and so Malcolmson then and there told in minute detail all that had happened in the last two nights. He was interrupted every now and then by some exclamation from Mrs Witham, till finally when he told of the episode of the Bible the landlady's pent-up emotions found vent in a shriek; and it was not till a stiff glass of brandy and water had been administered that she grew composed again. Dr Thornhill listened with a face of growing gravity, and when the narrative was complete and Mrs Witham had been restored he asked:

'The rat always went up the rope of the alarm bell?'

'Always.'

'I suppose you know,' said the Doctor after a pause, 'what the rope is?'

'No!'

'It is,' said the Doctor slowly, 'the very rope which the hangman used for all the victims of the Judge's judicial rancour!' Here he was interrupted by another scream from Mrs Witham, and steps had to be taken for her recovery. Malcolmson having looked at his watch, and found that it was close to his dinner hour, had gone home before her complete recovery.

When Mrs Witham was herself again she almost assailed the Doctor with angry questions as to what he meant by putting such horrible ideas into the poor young man's mind. 'He has quite enough there already to upset him,' she added. Dr Thornhill replied:

'My dear madam, I had a distinct purpose in it! I wanted to draw his attention to the bell rope, and to fix it there. It may be that he is in a highly overwrought state, and has been studying too much, although I am bound to say that he seems as sound and healthy a young man, mentally and bodily, as ever I saw – but then the rats – and that suggestion of the devil.' The doctor shook his head and went on. 'I would have offered to go and stay the first night with him but that I felt sure it would have been a cause of offence. He may get in the night some strange fright or hallucination; and if he does I want him to pull that rope. All alone as he is it will give us warning, and we may reach him in time to be of service. I shall be sitting up pretty late to-night and shall keep my ears open. Do not be alarmed if Benchurch gets a surprise before morning.'

'Oh, Doctor, what do you mean? What do you mean?'

'It is,' said the Doctor slowly, 'the very rope which the hangman used for all the victims of the Judge's judicial rancour!'

'I mean this; that possibly – nay, more probably – we shall hear the great alarm bell from the Judge's House to-night,' and the Doctor made about as effective an exit as could be thought of.

When Malcolmson arrived home he found that it was a little after his usual time, and Mrs Dempster had gone away – the rules of Greenhow's Charity were not to be neglected. He was glad to see that the place was bright and tidy with a cheerful fire and a well-trimmed lamp. The evening was colder than might have been expected in April, and a heavy wind was blowing with such rapidly-increasing strength that there was every promise of a storm during the night. For a few minutes after his entrance the noise of the rats ceased; but so soon as they became accustomed to his presence they began again. He was glad to hear them, for he felt once more the feeling of companionship in their noise, and his mind ran back to the strange fact that they only ceased to manifest themselves when that other – the great rat with the baleful eyes – came upon the scene. The reading-lamp only was lit and its green shade kept the ceiling and the upper part of the room in darkness, so that the cheerful light from the hearth spreading over the floor and shining on the white cloth laid over the end of the table was warm and cheery. Malcolmson sat down to his dinner with a good appetite and a buoyant spirit. After his dinner and a cigarette he sat steadily down to work, determined not to let anything disturb him, for he remembered his promise to the doctor, and made up his mind to make the best of the time at his disposal.

For an hour or so he worked all right, and then his thoughts began to wander from his books. The actual circumstances around him, the calls on his physical attention, and his nervous susceptibility were not to be denied. By this time the wind had become a gale, and the gale a storm. The old house, solid though it was, seemed to shake to its foundations, and the storm roared and raged through its many chimneys and its queer old gables, producing strange, unearthly sounds in the empty rooms and corridors. Even the great alarm bell on the roof must have felt the force of the wind, for the rope rose and fell slightly, as though the bell were moved a little from time to time, and the limber rope fell on the oak floor with a hard and hollow sound.

As Malcolmson listened to it he bethought himself of the doctor's words, 'It is the rope which the hangman used for the victims of the Judge's judicial rancour,' and he went over to the corner of the fireplace and took it in his hand to look at it. There seemed a sort of deadly interest in it, and as he stood there he lost himself for a moment in speculation as to who these victims were, and the grim wish of the Judge to have such a ghastly relic ever under his eyes. As he stood there the swaying of the bell on the roof still lifted the rope now and again; but presently there came a new sensation – a sort of tremor in the rope, as though something was moving along it.

Looking up instinctively Malcolmson saw the great rat coming slowly down towards him, glaring at him steadily. He dropped the rope and started back with a muttered curse, and the rat turning ran up the rope again and disappeared, and at the same instant Malcolmson became conscious that the noise of the rats, which had ceased for a while, began again.

All this set him thinking, and it occurred to him that he had not investigated the lair of the rat or looked at the pictures, as he had intended. He lit the other lamp without the shade, and, holding it up, went and stood opposite the third picture from the fireplace on the right-hand side where he had seen the rat disappear on the previous night.

At the first glance he started back so suddenly that he almost dropped the lamp, and a deadly pallor overspread his face. His knees shook, and heavy drops of sweat came on his forehead, and he trembled like an aspen. But he was young and plucky, and pulled himself together, and after the pause of a few seconds stepped forward again, raised the lamp, and examined the picture which had been dusted and washed, and now stood out clearly.

It was of a judge dressed in his robes of scarlet and ermine. His face was strong and merciless, evil, crafty, and vindictive, with a sensual mouth, hooked nose of ruddy colour, and shaped like the beak of a bird of prey. The rest of the face was of a cadaverous colour. The eyes were of peculiar brilliance and with a terribly malignant expression. As he looked at them, Malcolmson grew cold, for he saw there the very counterpart of the eyes of the great rat. The lamp almost fell from his hand, he saw the rat with its baleful eyes peering out through the hole in the corner of the picture, and noted the sudden cessation of the noise of the other rats. However, he pulled himself together, and went on with his examination of the picture.

The Judge was seated in a great high-backed carved oak chair, on the right-hand side of a great stone fireplace where, in the corner, a rope hung down from the ceiling, its end lying coiled on the floor. With a feeling of something like horror, Malcolmson recognised the scene of the room as it stood, and gazed around him in an awe-struck manner as though he expected to find some strange presence behind him. Then he looked over to the corner of the fireplace – and with a loud cry he let the lamp fall from his hand.

There, in the Judge's arm-chair, with the rope hanging behind, sat the rat with the Judge's baleful eyes, now intensified and with a fiendish leer. Save for the howling of the storm without there was silence.

The fallen lamp recalled Malcolmson to himself. Fortunately it was of metal, and so the oil was not spilt. However, the practical need of attending to it settled at once his nervous apprehensions. When he had turned it out, he wiped his brow and thought for a moment.

'This will not do,' he said to himself. 'If I go on like this I shall become a crazy fool. This must stop! I promised the Doctor I would not take tea. Faith, he was pretty right! My nerves must have been getting into a queer state. Funny I did not notice it. I never felt better in my life. However, it is all right now, and I shall not be such a fool again.'

Then he mixed himself a good stiff glass of brandy and water and resolutely sat down to his work.

It was nearly an hour when he looked up from his book, disturbed by the sudden stillness. Without, the wind howled and roared louder than ever, and the rain drove in sheets against the windows, beating like hail on the glass; but within there was no sound whatever save the echo of the wind as it roared in the great chimney, and now and then a hiss as a few raindrops found their way down the chimney in a lull of the storm. The fire had fallen low and had ceased to flame, though it threw out a red glow. Malcolmson listened attentively, and presently heard a thin, squeaking noise, very faint. It came from the corner of the room where the rope hung down, and he thought it was the creaking of the rope on the floor as the swaying of the bell raised and lowered it. Looking up, however, he saw in the dim light the great rat clinging to the rope and gnawing it. The rope was already nearly gnawed through – he could see the lighter colour where the strands were laid bare. As he looked the job was completed, and the severed end of the rope fell clattering on the oaken floor, whilst for an instant the great rat remained like a knob or tassel at the end of the rope, which now began to sway to and fro. Malcolmson felt for a moment another pang of terror as he thought that now the possibility of calling the outer world to his assistance was cut off, but an intense anger took its place, and seizing the book he was reading he hurled it at the rat. The blow was well aimed, but before the missile could reach it the rat dropped off and struck the floor with a soft thud. Malcolmson instantly rushed over towards it, but it darted away and disappeared in the darkness of the shadows of the room. Malcolmson felt that his work was over for the night, and determined then and there to vary the monotony of the proceedings by a hunt for the rat, and took off the green shade of the lamp so as to insure a wider spreading light. As he did so the gloom of the upper part of the room was relieved, and in the new flood of light, great by comparison with the previous darkness, the pictures on the wall stood out boldly. From where he stood, Malcolmson saw right opposite to him the third picture on the wall from the right of the fireplace. He rubbed his eyes in surprise, and then a great fear began to come upon him.

In the centre of the picture was a great irregular patch of brown canvas, as fresh as when it was stretched on the frame. The background was as before, with chair and chimney-corner and rope, but the figure of the Judge had disappeared.

Malcolmson, almost in a chill of horror, turned slowly round, and then he began to shake and tremble like a man in a palsy. His strength seemed to have left him, and he was incapable of action or movement, hardly even of thought. He could only see and hear.

There, on the great high-backed carved oak chair sat the Judge in his robes of scarlet and ermine, with his baleful eyes glaring vindictively, and a smile of triumph on the resolute, cruel mouth, as he lifted with his hands a *black cap*. Malcolmson felt as if the blood was running from his heart, as one does in moments of prolonged suspense. There was a singing in his ears. Without, he could hear the roar and howl of the tempest, and through it, swept on the storm, came the striking of midnight by the great chimes in the market place. He stood for a space of time that seemed to him endless, still as a statue and with wide-open, horror-struck eyes, breathless. As the clock struck, so the smile of triumph on the Judge's face intensified, and at the last stroke of midnight he placed the black cap on his head.

Slowly and deliberately the Judge rose from his chair and picked up the piece of the rope of the alarm bell which lay on the floor, drew it through his hands as if he enjoyed its touch, and then deliberately began to knot one end of it, fashioning it into a noose. This he tightened and tested with his foot, pulling hard at it till he was satisfied and then making a running noose of it, which he held in his hand. Then he began to move along the table on the opposite side to Malcolmson, keeping his eyes on him until he had passed him, when with a quick movement he stood in front of the door. Malcolmson then began to feel that he was trapped, and tried to think of what he should do. There was some fascination in the Judge's eyes, which he never took off him, and he had, perforce, to look. He saw the Judge approach – still keeping between him and the door – and raise the noose and throw it towards him as if to entangle him. With a great effort he made a quick movement to one side, and saw the rope fall beside him, and heard it strike the oaken floor. Again the Judge raised the noose and tried to ensnare him, ever keeping his baleful eyes fixed on him, and each time by a mighty effort the student just managed to evade it. So this went on for many times, the Judge seeming never discouraged nor discomposed at failure, but playing as a cat does with a mouse. At last in despair, which had reached its climax, Malcolmson cast a quick glance round him. The lamp seemed to have blazed up, and there was a fairly good light in the room. At the many rat-holes and in the chinks and crannies of the wainscot he saw the rats' eyes; and this aspect, that was purely physical, gave him a gleam of comfort. He looked around and saw that the rope of the great alarm bell was laden with rats. Every inch of it was covered with them, and more and more were pouring through the small circular hole in the ceiling whence it emerged, so that with their weight the bell was beginning to sway.

Hark! It had swayed till the clapper had touched the bell. The sound was but a tiny one, but the bell was only beginning to sway, and it would increase.

At the sound the Judge, who had been keeping his eyes fixed on Malcolmson, looked up, and a scowl of diabolical anger overspread his face. His eyes fairly glowed like hot coals, and he stamped his foot with a sound that seemed to make the house shake. A dreadful peal of thunder broke overhead as he raised the rope again, whilst the rats kept running up and down the rope as though working against time. This time, instead of throwing it, he drew close to his victim, and held open the noose as he approached. As he came closer there seemed something paralysing in his very presence, and Malcolmson stood rigid as a corpse. He felt the Judge's icy fingers touch his throat as he adjusted the rope. The noose tightened – tightened. Then the Judge, taking the rigid form of the student in his arms, carried him over and placed him standing in the oak chair, and stepping up beside him, put his hand up and caught the end of the swaying rope of the alarm bell. As he raised his hand the rats fled squeaking, and disappeared through the hole in the ceiling. Taking the end of the noose which was round Malcolmson's neck he tied it to the hanging bell-rope, and then descending pulled away the chair.

When the alarm bell of the Judge's House began to sound a crowd soon assembled. Lights and torches of various kinds appeared, and soon a silent crowd was hurrying to the spot. They knocked loudly at the door, but there was no reply. Then they burst in the door, and poured into the great dining-room, the doctor at the head.

There at the end of the rope of the great alarm bell hung the body of the student, and on the face of the Judge in the picture was a malignant smile.

'The Judge's House' was first published in *Holly Leaves* in December 1891. It was reprinted in the 1914 collection of short stories, *Dracula's Guest and Other Weird Stories*.

DUBLIN DIRECTORY

Note: Many of the sites listed in this directory are privately owned and may have specialised or seasonal hours, and require advanced booking. It is advised that you check with all sites before visiting them. Also, many civic museums are closed on Mondays.

CHURCHES

Rathfarnham Parish Church
(Page: 152)
Rathfarnham Village, Dublin 14
+353 1 409 5543

St. Anne's Church
(Page: 109)
Dawson Street, Dublin 2
+353 1 676 7727

St. John the Baptist's Church
(Page: 98)
Castle Road, Clontarf
+353 1 672 3370
1 April – 15 Oct: 10am to 7pm
16 Oct – 31 March: 10am to 4pm

St. Laurence Church
(Page: 59)
Chapelizod
+353 1 455 5639
Sunday 11am-12pm

St. Luke's Church
(Page: 31)
The Coombe, Dublin 8
Closed to the public

St. Mary's Chapel of Ease
(Page: 57)
St. Mary's Place, Dublin 1
Closed to the public

St. Michan's Church
(Page: 125)
Church Street, Dublin 7
+353 1 872 4154
Admission Charge

St. Patrick's Cathedral
(Page: 27)
St. Patrick's Close, Dublin 8
+353 1 453 9472
Admission Charge
www.stpatrickscathedral.ie
Virtual tour available on website

The Whitefriar Street Church
(Page: 26)
56 Aungier Street, Dublin 2
+ 353 1 475 8821
www.carmelites.ie

INSTITUTIONS

Clontarf Castle Hotel
(Page: 99)
Castle Avenue, Clontarf
+353 1 833 2321
www.clontarfcastle.ie

Crypt Arts Centre
(Page: 112)
Dublin Castle, Dublin 2
+353 1 671 3387
www.cryptartscentre.org

Dublin Castle
(Page: 110)
Cork Hill, Dublin 2
+353 1 677 7129
Admission Charge
www.dublincastle.ie
Virtual tour available on website

Dublin Tourist Office
Suffolk St., Dublin 2
+353 1 605 7700
www.visitdublin.com

Grand Lodge of Freemasons of Ireland
(Page: 18)
17 Molesworth Street, Dublin 2
+353 1 676 1337
www.irish-freemasons.org
Virtual tour available on website

Gaiety Theatre
(Page: 115)
South King Street, Dublin 2
Box Office: +353 1 677 1717
www.gaietytheatre.net
Virtual tour available on website

The Harcourt Hotel
(Page: 119)
60 Harcourt Street, Dublin 2
+353 1 478 3677
www.harcourthotel.ie

Leixlip Town Council
(Page: 36)
Newtown House
41 Captain's Hill
Leixlip, Co. Kildare
+353 1 624 5777
kildare.ie/leixlip

Royal College of Surgeons
(Page: 116)
123 St. Stephen's Green West
+353 1 402 2100
www.rcsi.ie
Virtual tour available on website

The Shelbourne Hotel
(Page: 122)
27 St. Stephen's Green North
+353 1 663 4500
www.shelbourne.ie
Virtual tour available on website

Trinity College
(Pages: 16, 62, 102)
College Green, Dublin 2
+353 1 608 1000
www.tcd.ie
Virtual tour available on website

Museums & Galleries

The Bram Stoker Dracula Experience
(Page: 99)
In the West Wood Club
Clontarf Road, Dublin 2
+353 1 805 7824
Admission Charge
www.thebramstokerdraculaexperience.
com

The Casino At Marino
(Page: 100)
Malahide Road, Marino
+353 1 833 1618

Chester Beatty Library
(Page: 112)
Dublin Castle, Dublin 2
+353 1 407 0750
www.cbl.ie

Dublin City Zoo
(Page: 58)
Phoenix Park, Dublin 8
+353 1 474 8900
Admission Charge
www.dublinzoo.ie
Virtual tour available on website

Dublin Writers Museum
(Page: 101)
18 Parnell Square North, Dublin 1
+353 1 872 2077
Admission Charge
www.writersmuseum.com

Leixlip Castle
(Page: 33)
Leixlip, Co. Kildare
Seasonal hours only
www.kildare.ie/leixlip/

Marsh's Library
(Page: 29)
St. Patrick's Close, Dublin 8
+353 1 454 3511
Admission Charge
www.marshlibrary.ie

National Gallery of Ireland
(Page: 63)
Merrion Square West, Dublin 2
+353 1 661 5133
www.nationalgallery.ie

National Library of Ireland
(Page: 108)
Kildare Street, Dublin 2
+353 1 603 0200
www.nli.ie

National Museum of Ireland
Archaeology & History
(Page: 108)
Kildare Street, Dublin 2
+353 1 677 7444
www.museum.ie

National Heraldic Museum of Ireland
(Page: 107)
2 Kildare Street, Dublin 2
+353 1 603 0311
www.nli.ie

Natural History Museum of Ireland
(Page: 66)
Merrion Square West, Dublin 2
+353 1 677 7444
www.museum.ie

The Newman House
(Page: 124)
85-86 St. Stephen's Green, Dublin 2
+353 1 706 7422

One Merrion Square
(Page: 105)
1 Merrion Square North, Dublin 2
+353 1 662 0281
Advanced booking essential
Admission Charge
www.amcd.ie

Pearse Street Library
(Page: 147)
138-144 Pearse Street, Dublin 2
+353 1 674 4888
www.dublincitypubliclibraries.ie

Number 29
(Page: 15)
29 Fitzwilliam Street Lower, Dublin 2
+353 1 702 6165
Admission Charge

The Wonderful Barn
(Page: 36)
Off Hillcrest Road, Leixlip
Co. Kildare

PARKS

Chaloner Cemetery
(Page: 16)
Trinity College, Dublin 2

The Garden of Remembrance
(Page: 101)
Parnell Square, Dublin 1

The Hell-Fire Club Lodge
(Page: 37)
Mount Pelier
Off Killakee Road

Iveagh Gardens
(Page: 119)
Clonmel Street, Dublin 2
Closes earlier than Dublin City parks

Le Fanu Park, 'The Lawns'
(Page: 61)
Ballyfermot

Marino Crescent Park
(Page: 97)
Marino Crescent, Clontarf

Merrion Square Park
(Page: 106)
Merrion Square, Dublin 2

Mount Jerome Cemetery
(Page: 71)
Harold's Cross Road, Harold's Cross
Closes promptly at 4pm

Phoenix Park
(Page: 58)
Conygham Road, Dublin 8

St. Kevin's Park
(Page: 68)
Camden Street, Dublin 2

St. Stephen's Green
(Page: 19)
City Centre, Dublin 2

PUBS & RESTAURANTS

The Bleeding Horse
(Page: 69)
24 Camden Street Upper, Dublin 2
+353 1 475 2705

Bram's Café
(Page: 99)
4 St. Aidan's Road, Fairview
+353 1 833 5610

Buswell's Hotel and Bar
(Page: 18)
25 Molesworth Street, Dublin 2
+353 1 614 6500

J.J. Smyth's
(Page: 68)
12 Aungier Street, Dublin 2
+353 1 475 2565

Mullingar House
(Page: 60)
Chapelizod Village, Dublin 20
+353 1 620 8692

Saagar Indian Cuisine
(Page: 119)
16 Harcourt Street, Dublin 2
+353 1 475 5012

The Swan Bar
(Page: 67)
57 Aungier Street, Dublin 2
+353 1 475 2722
www.swanbar.com

SHOPS

Bewley's Oriental Café
(Page: 103)
78 Grafton Street, Dublin 2
+353 1 816 0601
www.bewleys.com

Cathach Books
(Page: 110)
10 Duke Street, Dublin 2
+353 1 671 8676
www.rarebooks.ie

Eason's Bookshop
(Page: 105)
1 Dawson St., Dublin 2
www.eason.ie

Greene's Bookshop
(Page: 64)
16 Clare Street, Dublin 2
+353 1 676 2554
www.greenesbookshop.com

TOURS

The Dublin Experience
(Page: 17)
Trinity College, Dublin 2
+353 1 608 1000
Admission Charge
www.tcd.ie

Dublin Ghost Bus Tour
(Page: 74)
59 O'Connell Street, Dublin 1
+353 1 873 4222
Advance booking essential
Admission Charge
www.dublinbus.ie

Historical Walking Tours of Dublin
Meet at Trinity College front gates
+353 1 878 0227
Admission Charge
www.historicalinsights.ie

The Dublin Literary Pub Crawl
Meet at The Duke
9 Duke Street, Dublin 2
+353 1 670 5602
Admission Charge
www.dublinpubcrawl.com

Zozimus Experience
(Page: 112)
Meet at Dublin Castle gates
Advanced booking essential
Admission Charge
+353 1 661 8646
www.zozimus.com

TRAVEL

Dublin Area Rapid Transit (DART)
(Page: 74)
+353 1 703 3592
www.dart.ie

Dublin Bus
(Page: 11)
+353 1 872 0000
www.dublinbus.ie

Pat Liddy's Walking Tours of Dublin
(Page: 9)
Advanced booking essential
+353 1 831 1109
Admission charge
www.walkingtours.ie

West Suburban Rail
(Page: 36)
+353 1 703 3592
www.irishrail.ie

FURTHER INFORMATION

A wealth of information about gothic writers, including stories, articles, bibliographies and links to related sites, can be found at Jack Voller's excellent website: www.litgothic.com

Those willing to travel to Dublin may be interested in the Leslie Shepard Bram Stoker collection, a library of Bram Stoker-related books and tracts donated to the Dublin City Library and Archive by the late Stoker scholar Leslie Shepard. The Pearse Street Library is located at 138-144 Pearse Street, Dublin 2. More information can be found at: www.dublincitypubliclibraries.ie

There are also many literary societies around the world with interests in Maturin, Le Fanu and Stoker. Most of these societies operate internationally and have an active internet presence.

The Bram Stoker Society, Ireland
E-mail: Albert Power (gothicalbert@eircom.net)
Web: www.brianjshowers.com/stokersociety.html

> Dublin-based Stoker scholar Leslie Shepard (1917-2004) founded the Bram Stoker Society in 1980, with David Lass and John Leahy. The society's aims were to encourage serious appreciation of Bram Stoker and his writings. *The Bram Stoker Society Journal* was published annually between 1989 and 2001; edited first by Richard Dalby, and later by Albert Power. Not dead, the Bram Stoker Society is properly regarded as resting in its native soil, with the potential to rise up and forage forth for new members. Those interested in the society or copies of the journal should contact Albert Power.

The Dracula Society, United Kingdom
P.O. Box 30848, London W12 0GY
E-mail: TheDraculaSociety@yahoo.com
Web: www.thedraculasociety.org.uk

> The Dracula Society was formed in 1973 and caters to lovers of *Dracula*, Bram Stoker and all things gothic. The society produces a quarterly newsletter, *Voices From the Vaults*, and often sponsors trips to places connected with *Dracula* and Stoker.

Irish Georgian Society, Ireland
74 Merrion Square, Dublin 2
Tel: +353 1 676 7053
E-mail: info@igs.ie
Web: www.irish-architecture.com/igs/

Irish Georgian Society, United States
7 Washington Square N., New York, NY 10003-6647
Tel: +1 212 254 4862
E-mail: igeorgian@aol.com
Web: www.irish-architecture.com/igs/

> The Irish Georgian Society aims to encourage an interest in and to promote the conservation of distinguished examples of architecture and the allied arts of all periods in Ireland. These aims are achieved through education and grants, planning participation, membership and fundraising.

The Ghost Story Society, Canada
P.O. Box 1360, Ashcroft, British Columbia, Canada V0K 1A0
Tel: +1 250 453 2045; Fax: +1 250 453 2075
E-mail: Barbara Roden (nebuly@telus.net)
Web: www.ash-tree.bc.ca/GSS.html

The Ghost Story Society was formed in 1988 to provide admirers of the classic ghost story with an outlet for their interest. The society offers members an opportunity to exchange thoughts and ideas through the regular publication of its bi-yearly journal, *All Hallows*, which contains articles, letters, reviews and fiction.

A Ghostly Company, United Kingdom
24 Rectory Lane, Armitage, Rugeley, Staffordshire WS15 4AN
Web: www.aghostlycompany.org.uk

A Ghostly Company is a society with a limited membership, currently set to 100 members. The society publishes a frequent newsletter, which appears five or six times yearly. The newsletter includes members' letters, book reviews, a section for book sales and wanted books, and other news concerning events.

The Gothic Literary Club, Ireland
Tel: +353 87 980 4234
E-mail: Jonathan Barry (jonathanbarry@eircom.net)

Established in 1999 by Jonathan Barry, the Gothic Literary Club is a vibrant and active group, which meets on a monthly basis, at a regular venue in Dublin City centre. Its purpose is to bring together like-minded lovers of ghostly lore to read and share views on a range of great ghost stories, traditional and modern. Members of the group include biographers, writers and editors, though the emphasis of the group is primarily on enjoyment rather than the academic.

Le Fanu Studies, United States
1701 Lobdell Ave., No. 32, Baton Rouge, LA 70806-8242
Tel: +1 225 925 2917
E-mail: Gary W. Crawford (gothicpt12@aol.com)
Web: www.jslefanu.com/lefanustudies.html

Le Fanu Studies (ISSN 1932-9598) invites essays on any aspect of the life and works of famous Victorian mystery and ghost story writer Joseph Sheridan Le Fanu (1814-1873). It also seeks essays about works of drama, literature and film related to Le Fanu. The journal appears twice yearly, in May and November.

The Vampire Empire, United States
(Formerly The International Count Dracula Fan Club)
E-mail: Jeanne Youngson (vempireprez@benecke.com)
Web: www.benecke.com/vampire.html

Formerly the Count Dracula Fan Club, the society changed its name to The Vampire Empire in 2000. Jeanne Youngson, president and founder of the society, is dedicated to the promotion of the study of *Dracula* and Bram Stoker.

ENDNOTES

1 James Clarence Mangan quoted in Lougy, p.33

2 Lougy, p.33

3 Balzac was such a fan of *Melmoth the Wander* that he wrote a sequel, *Melmoth Réconcilié* (1835).

4 *Douglas Jerrold's Shilling Magazine*, 1846

5 Kearns, p.59

6 Idman, p.6

7 Byrne, p.65 and St. Claire, pp.108-110

8 John Melmoth was not the only character from horror literature to attend Trinity College – Detective Thomas Malone, from H.P. Lovecraft's 'The Horror at Red-Hook' (1927) was also a Trinity alumnus.

9 Trinity College's Historical Society, still active today, also counts Joseph Sheridan Le Fanu and Bram Stoker among its former members.

10 Charles Maturin quoted in Idman, p.7

11 www.excavations.ie

12 Igoe, p.56

13 Lougy, p.14

14 Belford's *Oscar Wilde, A Certain Genius*, pp.5-6

15 For more information on the failed struggle to preserve Georgian Molesworth Street, see Kevin Corrigan Kearns's illuminating book *Georgian Dublin: Ireland Imperilled Architectural Heritage* (1983).

16 Byrne, p.66

17 Somervile-Large's *Dublin: The Fair City*, p.176

18 Another gallows stood on present day Merrion Row, only in those days it was known as Gallows Row. Those hanged at Gallows Row were taken to Misery Hill where they were left to hang for anywhere between six months and a year. Misery Hill, near the Grand Canal Docks, still bears its name to this day.

19 Francis, Chapter VI: Saint Stephen's Green

20 Bowers, p.92

21 Bennett, p.197

22 When Maturin sent *Bertram* to Lord Byron, he neglected to include his name and return address. Byron had to go through the pains of tracking down the absent-minded author before he could dispatch an advance on the play.

23 Charles Maturin quoted in Idman, p.126

24 *Douglas Jerrold's Shilling Magazine*, 1846

25 Harrison, p.30

26 Ibid

27 Idman, p.13

28 Lougy, p.80

29 Somervile-Large, *Irish Eccentrics*, p.153

30 Saint Valentine's relics were a gift from Pope Gregory XVI to Father John Spratt in 1836. Father Spratt established the Whitefriar Street Church in 1824, and was known for working with Dublin's poor, especially those from the Liberties district just west of Saint Patrick's Cathedral.

31 Idman, p.4

32 Ibid, p.5

33 Phrenology, the study of the skull and its relation to mental faculties and character traits, was still quite popular at that time.

34 Carleton, p.189

35 When Archbishop Marsh died, he remained close to the library that he built and loved. He is buried just outside in Saint Patrick's churchyard, near the wall of his library.

36 McCarthy, pp.26-27

37 Idman, p.278

38 Ibid, p.308

39 *Dublin University Magazine*, 1858

40 Igoe, p.260

41 from *The Milesian Chief*

42 Mr Guinness is of the same family that started one of Ireland's biggest businesses. Over the centuries the Guinness family has been responsible for restoring and preserving everything from Saint Stephen's Green to Saint Patrick's Cathedral. Continuing in that tradition, the current Mr Guinness not only lovingly restored Leixlip Castle to its present state, but also founded the preservationist organisation the Dublin Georgian Society.

43 Joyce, Chapter 34

44 The theme of immortality and ever-youthful paintings was later used with much more skill and deftness by Oscar Wilde in his short novel *The Picture of Dorian Gray* (1890).

45 Ibid, pp.123-124

46 Ashe, pp.60-62

47 Some versions of the story say that the child was crippled, or not a child at all, but rather a dwarf.

48 Loughy, p.15

49 Joseph Sheridan Le Fanu was not the first in his family to attain literary distinction. His great-uncle Richard Brinsley Sheridan (1751-1813) was a noted playwright and politician.

50 *Madam Crowl's Ghost and Other Tales of Mystery* (1923)

51 McCormack, p.4-5; Cox, p.9

52 Kearns, p.89

53 Even New York City's Central Park, by comparison, is only 850 acres.

54 'Ghost Stories of Chapelizod' (1851)

55 Chapters VIII and IX from *The House by the Churchyard* are sometimes published separately as 'Ghost Stories of the Tiled House'.

56 M.R. James's epilogue, *Madame Crowl's Ghost and Other Tales* (1923)

57 'Ghost Stories of Chapelizod' (1851)

58 *The House by the Churchyard* (1863)

59 'Ghost Stories of Chapelizod' (1851)

60 McBryde, p.144

61 Le Fanu's time in County Limerick influenced his 'Stories of Lough Guir' (1870) much in the same way Chapelizod influenced 'Ghost Stories of Chapelizod'. Lough Guir (Gur) is just south of Limerick.

62 For background information on the Tithe War, W.J. McCormack details this portion of the Le Fanus' lives in *Sheridan Le Fanu* (1980)

63 Begnal, p. 25

64 O'Connell Bridge was built in 1880. During Le Fanu's lifetime, the bridge was known as the Carlisle Bridge, which had been built in 1794.

65 George Brinsley Le Fanu quoted in Ellis, p.175

66 Oscar was born around the corner at 21 Westland Row.

67 McCormack, p.215

68 'An Account of Some Strange Disturbances in Aungier Street' (1853)

69 Ibid

70 www.swanbar.com

71 Though churches have been constantly on this site since the early thirteenth century.

72 Of course not all bodies were re-interred. The increase in demand for cadavers for medical research resulted in entrepreneurs known as Resurrectionists, who were known to visit Saint Kevin's on a regular, if illegal, basis to exhume bodies for the nearby Royal College of Surgeons on Saint Stephen's Green.

73 The pub supposedly takes its name from a wounded horse that strayed into the pub from the Battle of Rathmines in 1649.

74 E.F. Bleiler, noted scholar of Victorian literature, believed Le Fanu's 'A Chapter in the History of a Tyrone Family' (1839) to be a major influence on Charlotte Brontë's *Jane Eyre* (1846).

75 For an excellent account of the days preceding Le Fanu's death, please see Jim Rockhill's introduction to *Mr Justice Harbottle and Others* (2005).

76 Begnal, p.82
77 A letter from Emma Lucretia Le Fanu to Lord Dufferin quoted in McCormack, p.270
78 McCormack, p.270
79 Sir William Wilde (1815-1876), Oscar's father. Other notable people buried in Mount Jerome include poet George William Russell (Æ), painters Jack B. Yeats and Walter Osbourne, writers John Millington Synge and William Carleton, and members of the Guinness family.
80 Section C, plot 122, grant 399. Detailed maps of the cemetery are available in the main office. It may be worth pointing out that W.J. McCormack misidentified the Bennett/Le Fanu vault in his biography *Sheridan Le Fanu*. For a further explanation of this misunderstanding, I refer you to my article 'Mix-Up at the Boneyard' published in the online journal *Le Fanu Studies*, which can be found at: www.jslefanu.com/lefanumixup.html
81 Ibid, p.125
82 Honourable mention also goes to Samuel Taylor Coleridge's poem 'Christabel' (1816) and James Malcom Rymer's serialised novel *Varney the Vampire: or the Feast of Blood* (1845).
83 Also known as 'Hommy-Beg', the Manx writer to whom *Dracula* was dedicated.
84 Stoker's working notes for *Dracula* are kept at the Philip H. and A.S.W. Rosenbach Foundation Library in Philadelphia.
85 Charlotte Stoker quoted in Ludlam, p.26
86 Ibid
87 There is confusion amongst Stoker's biographers as to exactly where Stoker lived and for how long. The addresses in this tour have been cross-referenced with as many sources as possible and verified with *Thom's Street Directory*. After careful research, the most accurate account of Stoker's movements whilst in Dublin come from Haining and Tremayne's book *The Un-Dead* (1998).
88 Oscar Wilde quoted in Ludlam, p.48
89 See Edgar Allan Poe's 'The Fall of the House of Usher' (1839)
90 Many scholars believe that the school was run by Reverend Wood. Haining and Tremayne point out that, while Wood was not the headmaster at the time Stoker attended the college, he may have been a teacher.
91 Parnell Square, in Stoker's time, was known as Rutland Square, while O'Connell Street was called Sackville Street, hence Oliver St John Gogarty's memoir *As I Was Going Down Sackville Street* (1937). Incidentally, Gogarty was born at 5 Parnell Square, which is now the Charles Stewart Hotel.
92 Bram's elder brother William 'Thornley' Stoker was known throughout his life simply as Thornley.
93 Belford, p.19
94 Incidentally, it may be worth noting that this image of Dracula is the first known published illustration of the infamous Count.
95 Belford, p.30
96 Haining and Tremayne, p.26
97 Belford, p.31
98 Ibid, p.30
99 Stoker, *Personal Reminiscences of Henry Irving* (1906)
100 Belford, pp.59-60
101 Belford, *Oscar Wilde: A Certain Genius*, pp.10-11
102 *Irish Popular Superstitions* (1852), *Ireland, Past, Present; the Land and the People* (1864) and *On the Ancient Races of Ireland* (1874).
103 Stoker got the name 'Dracula' from William Wilkinson's *An Account of Wallachia and Moldavia* (1820). It should also be noted that Stoker knew very little about Vlad Tepes, and did not base his Dracula on the historical Impaler. For more on this misconception, see Elizabeth Miller's illuminating *Dracula: Sense & Nonsense* (2000), Chapter Five: Vlad the Impaler.
104 For more information on the debate on whether or not 'Dracula's Guest' is an excised chapter from *Dracula*, please refer to Elizabeth Miller's *Dracula: Sense & Nonsense*, p.131-135.
105 'Dracula's Guest' (1914)
106 Barreca, p.32
107 www.club.ie

108 Shepard, Leslie. 'The Stoker Family on the Move', *The Bram Stoker Society Journal*, no.10, 1998.

109 Leatherdale, p.59

110 Belford, pp.85-86

111 Belford, p.34

112 Bram Stoker quoted in Belford, p.77

113 The Poddle River is now entirely underground, much like London's Fleet River. The only modern day evidence of the river is the small, grated outlet into the Liffey directly north of Dublin Castle, near the Capel Street Bridge, which can only be seen at low tide. There is also the matter of the entombed river's revenge when, after a heavy rain, it floods the basements of Dublin merchants who have set up shop over the tributary's final resting place.

114 Walter Osbourne, the famous Irish painter who painted a portrait of Florence Stoker, had a studio at this address.

115 Bram Stoker quoted in Farson, p.45

116 Abraham Stoker quoted in Farson, p.26

117 Haining and Tremayne, pp.94-95

118 Ibid, p.63

119 Ibid, p.82

120 Ibid, p.82

121 Stoker may also have been influenced by Joseph Sheridan Le Fanu's short story 'Mr Justice Harbottle' (1872). This is quite conceivable as he was certainly familiar with Le Fanu through his vampire novella 'Carmilla'. In fact, part one of 'Mr Justice Harbottle' is entitled 'The Judge's House'.

122 'The Judge's House' (1891)

123 Ibid

124 Miller, p.78

125 Haining and Tremayne, p.82

126 Gogarty, *As I Was Going Down Sackville Street*

127 Ibid

128 To be fair, it should be pointed out that the Stoker family believed this story to be a complete fabrication. It should also be noted that Gogarty subtitled his autobiography 'A Phantasy in Fact'.

129 Igoe, p.164

130 Sir William Wilde is buried in Dublin's Mount Jerome Cemetery. Abraham Stoker is interred in an English cemetery in La Cava, Italy.

131 Exactly how Irving influenced Stoker and his writing is disputed. Some scholars assert that it was Irving as a domineering employer or Irving as an object of homosexual desire. Dr Elizabeth Miller believes that Irving as an actor was a main influence – especially his role as Mephistopheles.

132 Neal's Music Hall on Fishamble Street has since been torn down, though a memorial marker has been erected to commemorate the debut of one of the world's most influential pieces of music.

133 When Charlotte moved back to Dublin from Italy following the death of her husband, she was a parishioner of the Rathfarnham Parish Church. There is a plaque in the church commemorating Abraham Stoker: 'For 50 Years in the Irish Civil Service, Dublin Castle...Beloved and Respected by All who Knew Him for his Many and Great Virtues.' Charlotte died on 15 March 1901.

134 Miller, p.96

135 One version of the story holds that Stoker caught syphilis in a Paris brothel when he went there to lend money to the destitute Oscar Wilde.

BIBLIOGRAPHY & SELECTED READING

CHARLES MATURIN

PUBLISHED WORKS

Fatal Revenge; or, The Family of Montorio. London: Longman, Hurst, Rees, and Orme, 1807.
The Wild Irish Boy. London: Longman, Hurst, Rees, and Orme, 1808.
The Milesian Chief. London: Henry Colburn, 1812.
Bertram; or, The Castle of St. Aldobrand. London: John Murray, 1816.
Manuel: A Tragedy. London: John Murray, 1817.
Women; or, Pour et Contre. London: Longman, Hurst, Rees, and Orme, 1818.
Fredolfo: A Tragedy. London: Constable and Co., 1819.
Sermons. London: Longman, Hurst, Rees, and Orme, 1819.
Melmoth the Wanderer. Edinburgh: Constable and Co., 1820.
The Albigenses. London: Hurst, Robinson and Co., 1824.
Five Sermons on the Errors of the Roman Catholic Church. Dublin: Folds, 1824.

BIOGRAPHICAL

Idman, Niilo. *Charles Robert Maturin: His Life and Works*. London: Constable and Co., 1923.
Kramer, Dale. *Charles Robert Maturin*. New York: Twayne, 1973.
Rathford, Fannie E., Wm. H. McCarthy Jr. (eds.). *The Correspondence of Sir Walter Scott and Charles Robert Maturin*. Austin: University of Texas, 1937.

CRITICISM

Axton, W.F. 'Charles Robert Maturin', *Supernatural Fiction Writers: Fantasy and Horror, volume 1*, edited by E.F. Bleiler. New York: Charles Scribner's and Sons, 1985.
Harris-Fain, Darren. *Dictionary of Literary Biography, Volume 178: British Fantasy and Science-Fiction Writers Before World War I*. Belmont: The Gale Group, 1997.
Lougy, Robert E. *Charles Robert Maturin – Irish Writers Series*. Lewisburg: Bucknell University Press, 1971.

Joseph Sheridan Le Fanu

Published Works

The Cock and the Anchor being a Chronicle of Old Dublin City. Dublin: William Curry, 1845.

The Fortunes of Colonel Torlogh O'Brien; A Tale of the Wars of King James. Dublin: James McGlashan, 1847.

Ghost Stories and Tales of Mystery. Dublin: James McGlashan, 1851.

The House by the Churchyard. London: Tinsley Brothers, 1863.

Wylder's Hand: A Novel. London: Richard Bentley, 1864.

Uncle Silas: A Tale of Bartram-Haugh. London: Richard Bentley, 1864.

The Prelude, Being a Contribution towards a History of the Election for the University, by John Figwood Esq., Barrister at Law (pseudonym). Dublin: G. Herbert, 1865.

Guy Deverell. London: Richard Bentley, 1865.

All in the Dark. London: Richard Bently, 1866.

The Tenants of Malory; a Novel. London: Tinsley Brothers, 1867.

A Lost Name, London: Richard Bently, 1868.

Haunted Lives; a Novel. London: Tinsley Brothers, 1868.

The Wyvern Mystery; a Novel. London: Tinsley Brothers, 1869.

Checkmate. London: Hurst and Blackett, 1871.

Chronicles of Golden Friars. London: Richard Bentley, 1871.

In a Glass Darkly. London: Richard Bentley, 1872.

Willing to Die. London: Hurst and Blackett, 1873.

The Purcell Papers. London: Richard Bentley, 1880.

The Poems of Joseph Sheridan Le Fanu. London: Downey, 1896.

Madame Crowl's Ghost and Other Tales of Mystery. Edited by M.R. James. London: G. Bell and Sons, Ltd., 1923.

Schalken the Painter and Others. Edited and introduced by Jim Rockhill, Ashcroft: Ash-Tree Press, 2002 (The complete supernatural tales volume 1).

The Haunted Baronet and Others. Edited and introduced by Jim Rockhill, Ashcroft: Ash-Tree Press, 2003 (The complete supernatural tales, volume 2).

Mr Justice Harbottle and Others. Edited and introduced by Jim Rockhill, Ashcroft: Ash-Tree Press, 2005 (The complete supernatural tales, volume 3).

Biographical

Crawford, Gary William. *J. Sheridan Le Fanu: A Bio-Bibliography (Bio-Bibliography in World Literature, No. 3)*. Westwood: Greenwood Publishing Group, February 1995.

McCormack, W.J. *Sheridan Le Fanu*. Oxford: Oxford University Press, 1980.

Criticism

Begnal, Michael H. *Joseph Sheridan Le Fanu – Irish Writers Series*. Lewisburg: Bucknell University Press, 1971.

Benson, E.F. 'Sheridan Le Fanu', *The Spectator* (February 1931).

Cox, Michael (ed.) *The Illustrated J.S. Le Fanu: Ghost Stories and Tales of Mystery by a Master Victorian Storyteller*. Wellingborough: Equation, 1988.

Ellis, S.M. *Wilkie Collins, Le Fanu, and Others*. London: Constable and Company, 1931.

BRAM STOKER

PUBLISHED WORKS

The Duties of Clerks of Petty Sessions in Ireland. Dublin: John Falconer, 1879.
Under the Sunset. London: Sampson Low, Marston, Searle, and Rivington, 1882.
The Snake's Pass. London: Sampson Low, Marston, Searle, Rivington, 1882.
The Watter's Mou'. London: Archibald Constable and Co., 1895.
The Shoulder of Shasta. London: Archibald Constable and Co., 1895.
Dracula. London: Archibald Constable and Co., 1897.
Miss Betty. London: C. Arthur Peterson, 1898.
The Mystery of the Sea. London: William Heinemann, 1902.
The Jewel of Seven Stars. London: William Heinemann, 1903.
The Man. London: William Heinemann, 1905.
Personal Reminiscences of Henry Irving, 2 vols. London: William Heinemann, 1906.
Lady Athlyne. London: William Heinemann, 1908.
Snowbound. London: Collier and Co., 1908.
The Lady of the Shroud. London: William Heinemann, 1909.
Famous Imposters. London: Sidgwick and Jackson, 1910.
The Lair of the White Worm. London: William Rider and Son, 1911.
Dracula's Guest and Other Weird Stories. London: George Routledge and Son, 1914.

BIOGRAPHICAL

Belford, Barbara. *Bram Stoker: A Biography of the Author of Dracula*. New York: Alfred A. Knopf, 1996.
Farson, Daniel. *The Man who Wrote Dracula: A Biography of Bram Stoker*. London: Michael Joseph, 1975.
Haining, Peter & Peter Tremayne. *The Un-Dead: The Legend of Bram Stoker and Dracula*. London: Trafalgar Square, 1998.
Ludlam, Harry. *A Biography of Dracula: The Life Story of Bram Stoker*. London: Fireside Press, 1962.
Murray, Paul. *From the Shadow of Dracula: A Life of Bram Stoker*. London: Jonathan Cape, 2004.
Shepard, Leslie. *Bram Stoker: Irish Theatre Manager & Author*. Dublin: Impact Publications, 1994. (Courtesy of the Estate of Leslie Shepard)

CRITICISM

Cahill, Anne (ed.) *The Newsletter of Stoker's Dracula Organisation: issues 1-10*. Dublin, 2000-2003.
Dalby, Richard & Albert Power (eds.) Bram Stoker Society Journal: vol. 1-13. Dublin: 1988-2001.
Leatherdale, Clive. *The Novel and the Legend: A Study of Bram Stoker's Gothic Masterpiece*. Wellingborough: The Aquarian Press, 1985.
Miller, Elizabeth. *Dracula: Sense and Nonsense*. Desert Island Books, April 2000, revised 2006.
Shepard, Leslie & Albert Power (eds.) *Dracula: Celebrating 100 Years*. Dublin: Mentor Press, 1997.

Miscellaneous

Ashe, Gregory. *The Hell-Fire Clubs: A History of Anti-Morality*. London: W.H. Allen & Co. Ltd., 1974.

Barreca, Regina (ed.) *Sex and Death in Victorian Literature*. London: Macmillan, 1990.

Bennett, Douglas. *The Encyclopaedia of Dublin*. Dublin: Gill and Macmillan Ltd., 1991.

Belford, Barbara. *Oscar Wilde: A Certain Genius*. New York: Random House, 2000.

Bowers, Moira. *Dublin City Parks & Gardens*. Dublin: The Lilliput Press, 1999.

Byrne, Patrick. *Irish Ghost Stories*. Dublin: The Mercier Press, 1971.

Carleton, William. *The Autobiography of William Carleton*. London: Macgibbon and Kee, 1968.

Gerard Francis. *Picturesque Dublin Old and New*. London: Hutchinson and Co., 1898.

Gogarty, Oliver St. John. *As I Was Going Down Sackville Street*. London: Rich and Cowan, Ltd., 1937.

Harrison, Wilmount. *Memorable Dublin Houses*. Dublin: W. Leckie and Co., 1890.

Igoe, Vivien. *Dublin Burial Grounds & Graveyards*. Dublin: Wolfhound Press, 2001.

Joyce, Weston St. John. *The Neighbourhood of Dublin*. 1912.

Kearns, Kevin Corrigan. *Georgian Dublin: Ireland's Imperilled Architectural Heritage*. London: David & Charles, 1983.

Lennon, Seán. *Irish Gothic Writers: Bram Stoker and the Irish Supernatural Tradition*. Dublin: Dublin Corporation Public Libraries, undated.

Lovecraft, H.P. *The Annotated Supernatural Horror in Literature*. Edited by S.T. Joshi. New York: Hippocampus Press, 2000.

McBryde, Gwendolen (ed.) *Letters to a Friend*. London: Edward Arnold Ltd., 1956.

McCarthy, Murial. *Marsh's Library: All Graduates and Gentlemen*. Dublin: Four Courts Press, 2003.

O'Donnell, E.E. *The Annals of Dublin: Fair City*. Dublin: Wolfhound Press, 1987.

Somerville-Large, Peter. *Dublin: The Fair City*. London: Stevenson-Sinclair, 1996.

Somerville-Large, Peter. *Irish Eccentrics: A Selection*. Dublin: Lilliput Press Ltd., 1999.

St. Claire, Sheila. *The Step on the Stairs: Paranormal Happenings in Ireland*. Dublin: The Glendale Press Ltd., 1988.

Thom's Official Directory etc, *Thom's Trade Directory*, *Thom's Law Directory* etc., Dublin: Alex Thom and Co. Ltd.

About the Author

Brian J. Showers is originally from Madison, Wisconsin, USA. He attended Madison's fine university and graduated in 1999 with a degree in English Literature and Communication Arts. His hobbies include writing and collecting comic books, reading tales of the supernatural, sampling local beers and exploring his environment – wherever he happens to be. He is a frequent contributor to The Ghost Story Society's journal *All Hallows*, and his short story 'The Old Tailor & the Gaunt Man' was published in Ash-Tree Press's award winning anthology *Acquainted With the Night*. Brian's ghost story chapbooks, illustrated by the unparalleled Duane Spurlock and the inimitable Meggan Kehrli, are available at on his website. Brian currently resides on the Emerald Isle, somewhere in the verdant and ghost-haunted wilderness of Dublin City, where he is busy at work on his first collection of ghost stories. More information can be found at: www.brianjshowers.com

'Literature and history influence place. Stories and locations stain a map with rich color in such a way that a brilliant picture is painted. Admission to see this priceless masterpiece is free to all those who stop and look at a map's shapes, textures and hues.

'When I moved to Dublin, I found myself on a new canvas. The longer I lived here, the more I learned. The more knowledge I collected, the clearer the picture became. Eventually, I accumulated enough details that I could barely walk two blocks without passing through a gallery of literature and history. I became a tour guide, not only for myself, but also for anyone who happened to be walking down the street with me.

'I am grateful for the opportunity to write a book on something I love, and would like to give special thanks to my friends and companions who at various times walked the streets with me, often holding the map so I would not get lost: Douglas A. Anderson, Mike Baron, Jonathan Barry, E.F. Bleiler, Peter Condell, Gary W. Crawford, John Crawford, Linda Eberle, 435 West Johnson Street, The Ghost Story Society, Jill Shepard Glenstrup, Damian Gordon, Desmond Guinness, Meggan Kehrli, David Lass, Pat Liddy, Murial McCarthy, Kerstin Mierke, Elizabeth Miller, Joe Mitchen, Noelle Moran, Mike Osbourne, David Pierpoint, Albert Power, Eoin Purcell and Nonsuch Ireland, Jim Rockhill, Barbara Roden, Christopher Roden, Bridgette Rowland, David E. Schultz, Gavin Selarie, Leslie Shepard, Ann Simmons, Duane Spurlock, Leo Tilson, Stephen Volk, Lucy Walshe, Gavin Woods, Anna-Lena Yngve, Josefin Yngve, my family, and anyone else I may have temporarily forgotten – you are not forgotten!'

Please direct all queries, comments and criticisms to the author at: gothicdublin@gmail.com

About the Illustrators

Except for three years as a bookseller, illustrator Duane Spurlock's professional career has centred on publishing – as a newspaper writer, editor-in-chief for software how-to journals, editorial director for internet publisher Emazing.com, and publications director in the health care field. He maintains The Pulp Rack (www.pulprack.com), which focuses on the popular fiction published in magazines during the first half of the twentieth century. He and his wife and their children live and garden, read and draw, and tell stories to one another in Kentucky. Duane may be reached at: pulprack@gmail.com

Meggan Kehrli is a graphic designer for a mid-sized technology firm in Chicago, that great metropolis somewhere between New York and Los Angeles. Her freelance work includes photography, linoleum block prints, hand-bound journals and Christmas cards. This is her first book cover and she would not mind doing a few more. Meggan can be contacted at: mkehrli@gmail.com

INDEX